T0314737

OLD SUSSEX INNS

OLD SUSSEX INNS

DONALD STUART

First published in Great Britain in 2005 by
The Breedon Books Publishing Company Limited
Breedon House, 3 The Parker Centre, Derby, DE21 4SZ.

This edition published in Great Britain in 2012 by The Derby Books Publishing
Company Limited, 3 The Parker Centre, Derby, DE21 4SZ.

ISBN 978-1-78091-189-2

Printed and bound by Copytech (UK) Limited, Peterborough.

Contents

Maps   6

A-Z of Old Sussex Inns   11

Maps of Highlighted Areas:

    Chichester   39

    Lewes   92

    Rye   128

    Steynings   143

MAP 1

A287

Fernhurst

Henley

Lodsworth

A272

Trotton

MIDHURST

Elsted

South
Harding

Didling

A3

Heyshott

Hooksway

Cocking

Compton

Chilgrove

West
Dean

Charlton

Walderton

East
Lavert

West
Ashling

A27

CHICHESTER

Chidham

Bosham

Merston

A259

Dell
Quay

Hunston

Sidlesham

Nyetimber

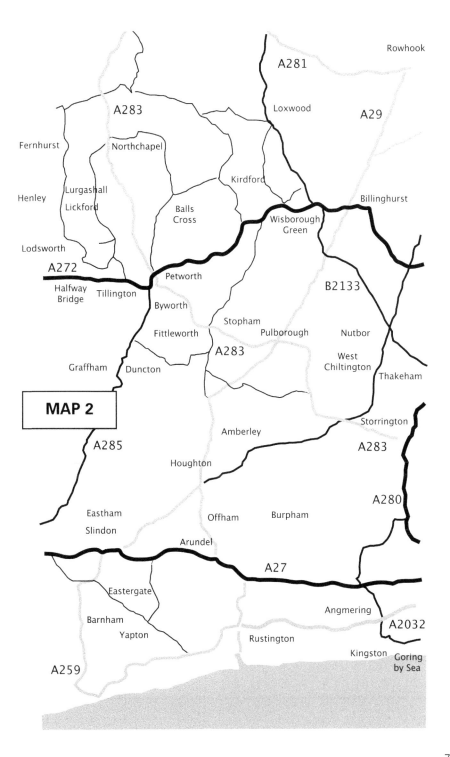

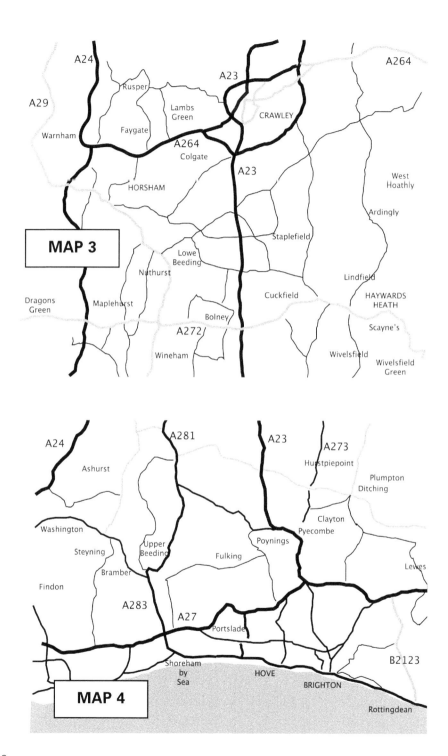

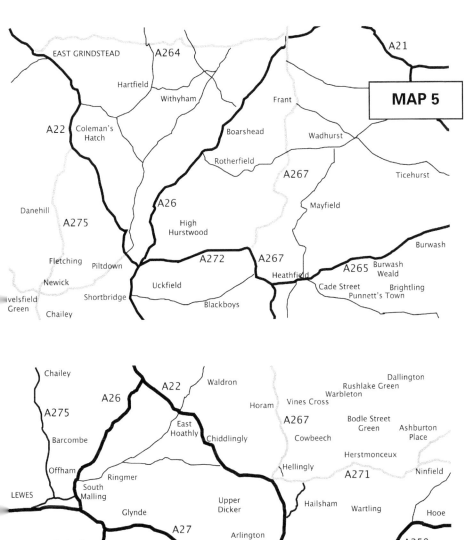

MAP 5

EAST GRINDSTEAD
A264
Hartfield
Withyham
Frant
A21
A22
Coleman's
Hatch
Boarshead
Wadhurst
Rotherfield
A267
Ticehurst
Danehill
A26
Mayfield
A275
High
Hurstwood
Fletching
Piltdown
A272
A267
Burwash
Newick
Uckfield
Heathfield
A265
Burwash
Weald
velsfield
Green
Shortbridge
Blackboys
Cade Street
Punnett's Town
Brightling
Chailey

MAP 6

Chailey
A22
Waldron
Dallington
Rushlake Green
A26
Horam
Vines Cross
Warbleton
A275
East
Hoathly
A267
Bodle Street
Green
Ashburton
Place
Barcombe
Chiddingly
Cowbeech
Offham
Ringmer
Hellingly
Herstmonceux
LEWES
South
Malling
A271
Ninfield
Glynde
Upper
Dicker
Hailsham
Wartling
Hooe
Rodmell
West
Firle
A27
Arlington
A259
Alciston
Polegate
Westham
Berwick
Wilmington
Pevens
NEWHAVEN
Denton
Alfriston
Lullington
Jevington
Willingdon
A2021
EASTBOURNE
A22
Seaford
A259
East
Dean

9

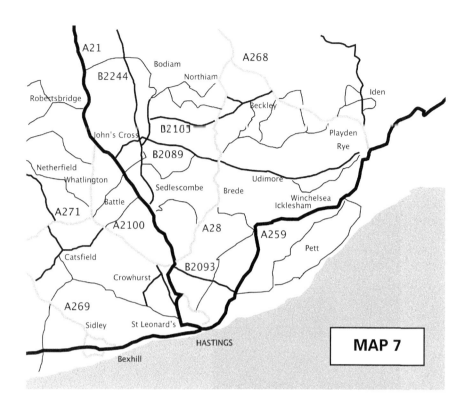

MAP 7

Alciston

(Map 6 page 9)

This village began life as the farm, or 'tun', of a Saxon called 'Aelfsige', so 'Aelfsige tun'. The nearby Court House farm has a 14th-century, 170ft long tythe barn. The word Bo-Peep was recorded at Alciston in the Turnpike Act of 1792 to refer to the turnpike keeper peering through his little window at travellers to make sure they paid. However, the first use was recorded in 1364 when Alice Cawston was forced to 'play bo-pepe thorowe a pillory' at Alciston for selling short measures of ale.

ROSE COTTAGE

Usually this pub name means tenants paid a peppercorn rent to the freeholder annually, which was traditionally either an amount of peppercorns, a root of ginger or one rose bloom. The building dates back to the 15th century and is built on two storeys with a steeply pitched roof. It is the last pub in the country where Good Friday skipping still takes place, after which it was traditional to go picking primroses. Skipping used to be a popular pastime in country areas and was part of fertility rites for the crops. The decor includes agricultural implements, stuffed birds and fish, a collection of old harnesses and Jasper, a noisy, African grey parrot. In the car park there are old enamel advertisements.

Alfriston

(Map 6 page 9)

Alfred the Great gave this farmstead and village to 'Aelfric' for services rendered. Alfriston was a seventh-century place of pilgrimage and has an early church where Saint Lewinna was buried after martyrdom in AD 690. Neolithic tribes lived nearby as evidenced by long barrows. The old village lock-up is in the car park.

GEORGE INN

The George Inn is a long building with half-timbering and it has been in business since 1397, when Whittington was Lord Mayor of London. In the past it was an important smuggling inn. It is a Grade I listed building with parts dating back to 1250, and inside there are deep fireplaces, heavy beams and wall frescos. During renovations in the 1930s, 16 layers of wallpaper were stripped to show the wall paintings. There is also a fine inn sign of wrought iron. Nearby, the location of the 14th-century village church resulted from a curious miracle. Four white oxen appeared on the village green and lay down forming a cross. The builders took this as a sign and built the church on that spot. Until a century ago, local shepherds were buried with a tuft of wool in their hands to prove to the Almighty that they had been working when they should have been in church on the Sabbath.

STAR

This was once a hospice for pilgrims on their way to Canterbury, but in the 1500s it became an inn. It has numerous wooden figures outside including a mitred abbot and Saint George and the Dragon. The red lion outside came from a Dutch naval ship that was wrecked in the 1800s. On the first floor, there are three oriel, leaded light windows. Legend has it that it was the Star Inn where Alfred the Great burned the cakes. Two ghosts have been seen here; one in mediaeval court-wear and the other dressed as a Victorian farmer. The farmer has been seen sitting in the lounge beneath the wall clock. One landlord awoke to see the old farmer walk across his bedroom, peer at something on the wall, turn around and walk back. He described him as being 60 years old with a floppy hat, old-fashioned smock with pleats in it and rough sack-cloth leggings tied with string. Several people have been locked in their rooms here and had to use the internal telephone to get released.

YE OLDE SMUGGLERS INNE and MARKET CROSS INN

This pub is over 600 years old, was once owned by smuggler Shanton Collins and is

said to be haunted by a seafaring gentleman and a farmer or shepherd. In 1744 Collins kidnapped revenue men who were bringing in a rescued cargo to Shoreham. He gave them a whipping and, when the booty was safely ashore, turned the boat back to France. Collins was eventually hanged for stealing sheep. At one time there were tunnels connecting houses with the inn but they were sealed up during World War One for security reasons. It has 20 rooms, 48 doors and six staircases. There is a 'devil's step' into a conservatory, beams with dried hops and butchers' hooks and an enclosed beer garden that is well favoured by walkers.

Amberley

(Map 2 page 7)

In Saxon 'Amber leah' meant a clearing by the river, and Amberley was recorded as 'Amberle' by AD 957. In AD 680 land was granted to St Wilfrid to build a church there by King Caedwalla.

AMBERLEY CASTLE HOTEL

Built nine centuries ago as a bishop's palace, Amberley Castle Hotel still has an oak portcullis that is brought down each night. There is a 12th-century Queen's Room and a Baronial Great Hall and the 14th-century walls and battlements enclose a garden. It is haunted by a young girl said to be Emily, a serving girl in the kitchens, who was seduced by a bishop in the 14th century. Now she wanders around, pale and sad, outside the old palace kitchens on the north side of the hotel.

BLACK HORSE

The Black Horse is an 18th-century inn overlooking a waterfall and the South Downs. It was once three cottages and has now been knocked into three bars that can be reached by a flight of steps, each containing many local relics. There is a collection of old sheep bells belonging to Frank Oliver, the last shepherd in the village. At one time there were several sheep bells used: the canister bell with the most musical sound, the clucket bell with a duller note that carried further and the rumbler bell with a ball inside that gave out a continuous note. On the door is written: 'Take note. It is forbidden for beggars, itinerant musicians and females of doubtful reputation to enter this pub'. (Dated May, 1907.)

BRIDGE INN

Situated below the hills of Amberley, near an ancient bridge and river crossing it, the Bridge Inn started life as a farmhouse in 1740, the same year 'Rule Britannia' was written by James Thomson. There was much industrial growth at the time as large supplies of chalk were cut for the building trade and shipped out by barge and rail. Close by is the Amberley Chalk Pits Museum, which has a wide range of exhibits from railway locomotives to brick-making and pottery. Not far from the pub a Saxon dug-out canoe was found, cut from a single tree, and it is now in the British Museum.

Angmering

(Map 2 page 7)

Angmering was a Saxon settlement built on a Roman site. A Roman villa was unearthed here in the 19th century, close to an Iron Age ditch some 2,500 years old. The Saxon name was 'Angemaeringas' and the village appeared under this name in AD 880.

LAMB

This has stood here as an inn for four centuries, and one fireplace has a Charles I style fireback dating from 1627. It is a large, old coaching inn in the centre of the village and it is surrounded by 18th and 19th-century houses, some thatched and others weatherboarded or flint-faced.

SPOTTED COW

Three centuries ago the Spotted Cow opened its doors and became home to smugglers. In one bar is the wheel, a ceiling mounted game, but the origins are vague. It has been suggested that this could have been a spinning jenny used by smugglers to divide their ill-gotten gains. An annual charity conkers-knockout event and hog roasts are held here. It is surrounded by trees on a country lane and has old-fashioned, green shutters.

Ardingly

(Map 3 page 8)

Ardingly's name derives from the Saxon word 'leah' meaning a cleared area of woodland. This was occupied by 'Eardingas', meaning Earda's people.

GARDENERS ARMS

The Gardeners Arms is a cottage-style pub, built outside the village in the early 1700s, with a number of bars. It was once a coaching inn with a courtroom, and parts of the building date back to the 12th century. Often these inns were built for market gardeners living nearby and sometimes carried the text, 'By the sweat of thy brow shalt thou eat bread'. Nearby is the South of England Showground, used for fairs, rallies and the big event in June.

OAK INN

The Oak has been a popular name for pubs for centuries and is often connected with royalty or the Royal Navy. It opened as an inn in 1625, at the time of Charles I, but

it was originally built 200 years previously as three labourers' cottages and was used as a meeting place for beaglers. It is heavily beamed and has a large, inglenook fireplace and built-in seats. There is a hunting horn in the bar that was taken to World War One to lead soldiers into battle. The ghost of a young girl has been seen regularly at 6pm, wearing a grey cloak with long dark hair, walking towards the inglenook fire and dissolving away.

Arlington

(Map 6 page 9)

In the 1300s, the church here was enlarged to shelter people escaping the black death and there are still remnants of mediaeval paintings inside. The village evolved from a farmstead that was owned by 'Eorla' or 'eorl', a nobleman or warrior.

OLD OAK INN

The Old Oak is a 17th-century inn with oak beams. It is part-panelled and has a wooden-floored bar and open log fires. Once it was a row of four almshouses, but one of the cottages became an alehouse used by charcoal burners from nearby Abbot's Wood. It was rebuilt in 1773, the year the Boston Tea Party made their revolutionary protest against British taxes. God-fearing locals once gave unusual names to their children such as 'No-merit Vinall' and 'God's Blessing Bell', recorded in the Arlington parish register. It is in a great area for picking bluebells in springtime.

YEW TREE INN

The Yew Tree Inn is a delightful country pub with a small animal farm. It is part-panelled and has bare wood floors, an open log fire and an unusual brick fireplace. The yew trees were of great significance in the Middle Ages as they were used to

manufacture bows. During the reign of Henry V, an act was passed to protect them and many can still be found in country churchyards.

Arundel

(Map 2 page 7)

Arundel comes from 'Hirondelle', the French word for swallow. Nearby is Knucker Hole, said to be bottomless and home to a strange serpent.

ST MARY'S GATE INN

Standing next to an imposing cathedral is St Mary's Gate Inn. It was built during the reign of Henry VIII. When in pursuit of Cavaliers, it was used as Roundhead headquarters. It once had a thatched roof and has previously been a farm

dwelling. In 1764 Henry Mackett, described as a tapsta (the name given to alehouse keepers), became landlord. In those days beer was served in jugs called 'Brown Georges'.

Ashburnham

(Map 6 page 9)

Once the centre of the Saxon iron industry, Ashburnham was known as 'aesc burna ham', the ash-bourne settlement. Nearby there are old earthworks that may be the lost town of Mercredsburn that was conquered by the Saxon Aella in AD 419. When Charles I was executed, in 1649, souvenirs were brought back and kept in the church here as they were believed to have healing properties. This included his shirt, silk drawers, garters, watch and a lock of hair. The last iron foundry in Sussex was put out here in 1813.

ASH TREE INN

Now four centuries old, the Ash Tree is red-brick and board with a tiled roof. It is one of 50 pubs in the area named after different trees and denotes a local connection. With four bars, open fires and a hedged garden, it is known as the 'little lost inn in the woods'. There is the most splendid garden, in which butterflies appear in the summertime, and a fantastic view.

Ashurst

(Map 4 page 8)

In the 13th century Ashurst was recorded as 'Asshehurst'. The village graveyard contains the body of Margaret Fairless Dowson (1869–1901) who, under the pseudonym Michael Fairless, wrote *The Roadmender*, a story about Sussex folk. In the local church there is a vamphorn, one of only six in the country, that was used to give musical pitch to singers.

FOUNTAIN INN

Four hundred years ago this building was used as a farmhouse. It overlooked a duck pond that still remains and now has a jetty over it for eating al fresco. Gentrified in Georgian times, a new façade was added to make it look really grand. The tap room has flagstones and an open fireplace and leads into a lounge bar. There is a huge inglenook fireplace in the small front bar. Several years ago, Paul McCartney and Wings used the pub to record their Christmas song, *Wonderful Christmas Time*. The pub was praised by Hilaire Belloc in *The Four Men*.

Balls Cross

(Map 2 page 7)

STAG

The Stag is over 400 years old and is a stone-built former coaching inn with stone floors. It has two small bars and a large inglenook fireplace. Found up a series of lanes, the pub is also the local polling station and is well used by walkers. A spit on which a sheep is roasted for the Horn Day festival, held annually for five centuries, is kept in the pub.

Barcombe

(Map 6 page 9)

Barley has always been a staple crop around Barcombe and the village name began as 'bere camp', meaning barley field, becoming 'Berecomb' by 1233, just before Cambridge University was granted a Royal Charter. A plaque on the road bridge shows that this was the first tollgate in the county, built in 1066.

ANCHOR INN

The Anchor is a remote inn that can found down a country lane that runs to the River Ouse. It was built for bargees in 1790, the year the *Bounty* Mutineers settled on Pitcairn, and was once the smallest pub in the south of England. At one time it was called the Fisherman's Rest and used by poachers to sell their ill-gotten gains, while one shed was being used as a slaughterhouse. The Anchor was known as a house of ill-repute and in 1894 Sir William Grantham bought it in order to take the licence away. It was a black market centre during World War Two. Some unusual ship's timbers and posts, taken from old windjammers, can be found in one bar. Boat hire is available and it also has a marriage licence.

Barnham

(Map 2 page 7)

Barnham is an old fishing village on the River Arun and was known as 'Beorna ham' which, in Saxon, meant the heroic one.

MURRELL ARMS

In 1981, for the wedding of Princess Diana and Prince Charles, a hopscotch pitch was set up outside the pub on the green and is still used by local children. This pub has to be seen to be believed as it has a large collection of memorabilia, ephemera and delightful items. (There is even, according to the landlady, a huge pair of tweezers for plucking elephants' eyebrows.) It is a traditional three-bar village pub, but there are fears that it may not be long before it will be vandalised to provide a mock horse-brass replica of a country pub. There is a complete history of the village on a board outside going back as far as William Murrell, Yeoman of Barnham (1718–91). Go and see it before it goes.

Battle

(Map 7 page 10)

Battle was recorded in the Domesday Book as 'La Batailge'. Isaac Ingall, who was butler at the abbey for 100 years and died in 1798 at the age of 120, is buried in Saint Mary the Virgin's churchyard and there is a memorial to Edmund Cartright here, the inventor of the power loom.

GEORGE HOTEL

An inn has stood here for 600 years. The present building is 18th-century and has been a town hall and courthouse. During the Napoleonic Wars the English militia were billeted here. Nearby there is the Great Abbey at Battle that was founded by William the Conqueror. From time to time here there is a 'Bloody Fountain' said to represent the vast amounts of Christian blood spilt at this place, and there are tales of King Harold appearing with an arrow in his head. The George is next door to the Old Pharmacy, which also dates from the 18th century.

KING'S HEAD

The King's Head is a 15th-century inn with features including an inglenook fireplace and low-beamed ceilings. Until fairly recently, it was known as Ye Olde King's Head. Guy Hayler, a founder of the Temperance Movement, was born nearby. Locally, there were workshops for manufacturing gunpowder from 1676.

It is surrounded by 17th and 18th-century houses and has King Harold on the inn sign.

Beckley

(Map 7 page 10)

Alfred the Great once owned this land and willed it to his kinsman, Osferthe. Originally the village was known as 'Beccan leah', meaning a woodland cleared by Becca.

ROSE AND CROWN

This pub opened in 1680, about the same time that oil lighting was introduced in London. It has an inglenook fireplace and a firefighting theme in the form of paintings and equipment. Late at night, the ghost of one of the knights who murdered Thomas Becket rides through this village and passes this pub. He had tried to gain sanctuary at the local church while still covered in blood from that infamous deed. The ghost, Sir William de Tracy, also appears at Woolacombe, Devon, riding his horse up and down the sands and howling. The local church houses a 12th-century chest, thought to have contained church treasure, with some of the oldest ironwork in the country binding it.

Berwick

(Map 6 page 9)

Edward III decreed that all men must practice archery on Sundays and at Berwick they sharpened the points of their arrows inside the church tower, the marks of which are still there near the font. Many archers who went to Crécy, Poitiers and Agincourt came from Berwick.

CRICKETERS

The Cricketers is a five centuries old, brick and flint pub with half-panelled walls, scrubbed tables and benches. Once it was two cottages plus an extension, which explains the different types of brick and stone faces. The bars are beamed and there is a large collection of antique cricket bats hanging on the walls. In the local

church are wall paintings by Vanessa Bell and Duncan Grant of the Bloomsbury Group.

Bexhill

(Map 7 page 10)

In AD 722, the village was recorded as 'Bexlea'. When the Saxons arrived they found Neolithic earthworks covered with box wood and so called it 'byxe leah', meaning box wood.

ROYAL SOVEREIGN

This is an early Victorian town pub that was named after several ships of the Royal Navy bearing this name. The last of these was a

1915 battleship, but the 17th-century *Royal Sovereign* was the most famous and was also known as Sovereign of the Seas. The name was also applied to a variety of strawberry and a brew once made by Kentish Ales.

Billingshurst

(Map 2 page 7)

Billingshurst was known as 'Billingas Hyrst', a Saxon wooded area that belonged to Billas's people. In 1203 it was recorded as 'Bellingsherst'.

KING'S ARMS

Set down below the level of the road, this pub is four centuries old and built in brick with hung-tiles. As it was once a coaching inn, there are buildings at the side and rear to accommodate horses and vehicles. There are two main bars with huge barrels used as tables and wooden flooring throughout. This small area dates back to Roman times and was known as Stane Street.

KING'S HEAD

Further up the road from the King's Arms is the King's Head that gave rise to a merry jest when two such named pubs were near each other. There is a story written by Charles Hindley in his *Tavern Anecdotes* about a courtier of King Charles II who asked a friend about a decent hostelry and was told: 'You will find the King's Arms are always full while the King's Head is empty.'

LIMEBURNERS ARMS

The Limeburners Arms is 400 years old and was once a row of three cottages lived in by the men who burned limestone in kilns to produce lime. It is a fine roadside inn on two storeys with red hung-tiles. Outside there is a campsite. A Charles II shilling was found under the floor of the bar here during renovation.

OLDE SIX BELLS

The building is a 15th-century coaching inn and has a clock half the size of the one at Westminster (Big Ben). It is a fine example of a timber-framed house with a Horsham stone roof. It has the longest stone-flagged floor in the country and one fireplace has a 16th-century gravestone as a fireback. Recently a tile-hung wall was opened to reveal a 16th-century window with original nails. There are several bars and a large garden with tables for al fresco eating.

Blackboys

(Map 5 page 9)

BLACKBOYS

This pub is over 600 years old and was named after Richard Blackboys, owner of the local estate in the 14th century, and also after the 'black boys' who were the charcoal handlers at the iron foundries in the 14th century. It is black and white weatherboarded, has alcove seats and overlooks the pond. There is an outside drinking area under a spreading chestnut tree. During the night, there have been footsteps heard here and a drop in temperature felt. It is said to be the ghost of Annie Starr, an 18th-century maid and daughter of the landlord, who became pregnant by a local aristocrat and was then abandoned. She is said to be looking for the man who betrayed her and the baby who died shortly afterwards. Cricket has been played on the village green here since the 18th century.

Boarshead

(Map 5 page 9)

This name came from animal sacrifices made in pagan times when the head of an animal was set up on a pole. The village was known as 'Boreshead' by 1556. Jack Fenner, who died here in 1979 aged 92, was the last maker of handmade edge-tools in England. One of the six bells at St Giles church here is dedicated to Haile Selassie as a previous vicar had been his aide-de-camp.

BOAR'S HEAD INN

The pub sign dates back to the 14th century when it was a Christmas custom to serve a boar's head with an apple or lemon in its mouth. It is still observed at Queen's College Oxford and 16th-century carols are sung as the dish is brought to the dining table. The pub has oak beams and an inglenook fireplace and it first opened in 1636, at the time of the first settlement of Rhode Island.

Bodiam

(Map 7 page 10)

Bodiam was on a main river-crossing point in Roman times. It has the last great mediaeval fortress in England, which was built between 1385 and 1390 to guard against French invaders. In Saxon it was known as 'Bodan hamm', the water meadow of Boda. Until recently it was pronounced 'Bodjum'.

CASTLE

Situated near Bodiam Castle, this inn moved from across the road in 1880 where it had been known as the Red Lion. It was originally built in the 14th century to provide food and lodgings for visitors to Bodiam Castle, which is said to be the finest ruined castle in the country. Bodiam Castle was rescued by Mad Jack Fuller of Brightling who bought it to prevent a firm of builders demolishing it. Inside the pub there is a large, log fireplace and outside, a boules pitch.

Bodle Street Green

(Map 6 page 9)

Named after the Bothel family during the 14th century, Bodle Street Green was known as 'Bodylstreet' in 1539 and 'Bodell Street' 50 years later.

WHITE HORSE INN

This name and symbol has been around for centuries and owes its popularity to heraldic use. It was used by the kings of Wessex and is also the emblem of Kent. It is on the arms of several guilds including carmen, farriers, innkeepers, saddlers and wheelwrights. The white horse is painted on the roof as well as being on the inn sign. The inn was rebuilt in about 1850, moving from its original site 50 yards away.

Bolney

(Map 5 page 9)

Bolney was called 'Bolleneye' by 1279, deriving from the Saxon name 'Bollan Eg', Bolla's Island, a firm ground surrounded by marshland. The church has a rare, full lychgate entrance. 'Lych' is Old English for corpse, and a body would stay under the gate until the vicar came for it.

BOLNEY STAGE

A stagecoach used to be parked outside this roadside inn built on the old main London–Brighton Road. The village is famous for its bells and bell-ringers, and it has been the custom, over the years, to stand by the village pond to hear the

reverberation of the bells coming off the water making them sound perfect. The village church is surrounded by fine 18th-century buildings.

Bosham

(Map 1 page 6)

Pronounced Bozzum, the name dates back to AD 750 from the name 'Bosan hamm', meaning the water meadow of Bosa. King Canute said that even he could not turn back the waves here; that was God's work. Canute's daughter, who died when she was eight years old, was buried in the local church and discovered in 1865. It is said that treasure was buried at the manor here during the English Civil War. During the time of the Great Plague the fishermen of Bosham left food outside the locked gates of Chichester for the local people and for this were waived their market fees in perpetuity.

ANCHOR BLEU

This waterside inn has stood here since 1740 and is mentioned in the *Schedule of Taverns*. It has one stone-flagged bar and one with close-boarded planks. It is low-beamed with timber props and is decorated with old nautical prints. At one time it was known as the Carpenter's and Cobbler's Arms. The Romans landed near this point and there is a quay nearby where 'boat people' now land for drinks and food. It was used by artist Rex Whistler and, later, the poet Dylan Thomas when it was said

that 'parties got out of hand'. At the end of the lane is a sausage shop, O'Hagans, that is well worth a visit.

Bramber

(Map 4 page 8)

In AD 956, the village was recorded as 'Bremre' deriving from the Saxon word 'bremer', meaning a thicket of broom. Nearby is St Mary's House, a 15th-century, timber-framed house built for the monks who were wardens of the bridge here.

YE CASTLE

On a hill above this inn is the ruined Bramber Castle that this hostelry was named after. Over 800 years ago, the castle was owned by William De Breose. King John questioned his loyalty and wanted to take his children as hostages. De Breose's wife and children fled to Ireland but were captured and taken to Corfe Castle, Dorset, where they starved to death. Lord De Breose is still remembered in Welsh folklore as the 'Ogre of Abergavenny' because of his extreme cruelty. The ghosts of the De Breose children are believed to be in Bramber and, usually around Christmas time, have been seen outside this inn looking up at the castle, begging for food and arrayed in ragged clothing. They disappear when spoken to.

Brede

(Map 7 page 10)

Brede is a small settlement on a river in a wide valley, which was called 'Braedu' because of its breadth.

RED LION

The Red Lion is a village inn with the most popular of inn names. Once there were 600 'Red Lions' throughout Britain named after the insignia of John of Gaunt, the most powerful man in England in the 14th century. In 1530 a customer was seen by the rector reading his psalter and as it was the English translation he was given four days in the stocks. The village is haunted by Sir Goddard Oxenbridge, the 'Brede

Giant', who carried off young children and ate them. Legend has it that he was caught by local children who got him drunk and sawed him in half using a wooden-toothed saw. His ghost haunts nearby Groaning Bridge. In the church here there is a carved Madonna by Sir Winston Churchill's cousin, Clare Sheridan. Captain Hook of *Peter Pan*, by J.M. Barrie, was based on a local vicar, Revd William Maher, a smuggler and churchman. In 1830 the labour rioters, led by Captain Swing, disliked the Brede workhouse keeper, Thomas Abell. The unfortunate Abell was tied to a dung cart and dropped over the parish boundary.

Brighton

(Map 4 page 8)

COLONNADE BAR, New Road
Next door to the Theatre Royal, this superb Edwardian-style bar is decorated in red plush, mirrors and photographs of actors who have appeared at the theatre over the years. Once the 'ladies of the night' paraded underneath the arches of this Georgian building. The theatre was opened in 1822 and was regularly visited by the Prince of Wales. It is haunted by a Grey Lady who has been described by many staff and actors who have seen her as being about five feet six inches tall, between 50 and 60 years old and of a commanding presence. (Danny la Rue insisted she had been trying on his wigs while he was out.) The bar itself is haunted by another Grey Lady who sits in a corner. One manager said, 'she was wearing a lovely grey chiffon dress. She was in no way frightening and, before I could say anything, with a sweet smile she disappeared. The odd thing was she did not seem to have any feet or ankles.'

Burpham

(Map 2 page 7)

Alfred the Great built a stronghold here against marauding Danes and by AD 920 it was known as 'Burhham', meaning the settlement beside the stronghold. Once there was a leper colony nearby and the Leper's Window at the church dates from 1330.

GEORGE AND DRAGON

The pub was connected with the smuggling trade and a spinning jenny, used to divide the loot, is still fixed to the ceiling. It opened in 1742, the same year as the first performance of Handel's *Messiah* in Dublin, on the site of an inn built 300 years earlier. It was owned by one family for many years up until 1945 when Ada and Gertrude West died. A niece of the sisters who died at the inn is still in residence and occasionally makes an appearance. There is a portrait of the dead girl hanging in the bar. Edward Lear (1812–1888), artist and author, lived nearby and wrote his *Book of Nonsense* here in 1846. Author Mervyn Peake is buried in St Mary's graveyard and while living in Burpham he wrote *Titus Groan*.

Burwash

(Map 5 page 9)

Burwash was once a fortified Saxon village known as 'Burh ersc'. It is now pronounced Berrish. Rudyard Kipling lived here, at Batemans, until he died in 1936, where he wrote *Puck of Pook's Hill*, *Rewards and Fairies* and *Traffics and Discoveries*.

BELL INN

Near to Kipling's home, owned by the National Trust, is this 17th-century brick, weatherboarded and tiled inn, originally built in the 15th century. It has log fires, a collection of old barometers and pew-style seats. Situated opposite the parish church, it is ivy-covered and set amid some fine ancient houses. Batemans was built by a local ironmaster and there is a watermill dating from 1750 in the grounds.

Burwash Weald

(Map 5 page 9)

WHEEL INN

When George II died in 1760, this pub opened as the Catherine Wheel, named after Saint Catherine who was martyred on a wheel. Pubs with such names usually denote wheelwrights working on stagecoaches and carts. It was a noted 'rough pub' when in 1834 some visitors described it as the roughest pub ever.

Home to smugglers and other criminals, there were constant battles between them and the revenue men. Outside there are a number of old iron wheels.

ROSE AND CROWN

The Rose and Crown was an Elizabethan coaching inn and has a large inglenook fireplace with wooden seats at each end. In the village centre there are 17th and 18th-

century houses, some thatched and others with mansard roofs. (A two-slope roof introduced by Mansard, a 17th-century French architect who was influenced by the Dutch.) Nearby is a building dating from the 1380s, which is now an antiques shop. The pub is low-beamed and has settles, a flagged courtyard, low doorways and lead-paned glass windows. Outside are the old coaching stables.

Byworth

(Map 2 page 7)

In 1279 this village had three names, 'Begworth', 'Beghworth' and 'Byworthe', from the Saxon 'Baegan woro', meaning Baegas's enclosure.

BLACK HORSE

An Elizabethan function room is a main feature of this pub, built in 1791 when the Ordnance Survey of Great Britain was established. It has wood panelling and old beams. Once a priory, it has a Georgian façade concealing an older structure and a cobbled patio.

Cade Street

(Map 5 page 9)

JACK CADE

In years gone by the April Heffle Cuckoo Fair was held here at the Half Moon Inn, now called the Jack Cade. In Saxon times this was known as Catte Street or, perhaps, Cart Street, as it was known as Cartestrete in 1330 and Kattestrete in 1288. It changed to Cade Street in the 1700s in memory of the leader of the 1450s revolt. Cade organised the Kentish rebellion and led an army to London. He was killed as they were leaving by Alexander Iden, Sheriff of Kent, and his head was put up on London Bridge.

Catsfield

(Map 7 page 10)

Catsfield was named after the 'Catti', a Saxon tribe, and also Saint Cedd who built a church here on land where feral cats lived. In 1086 it was known as 'Cedesfelle'.

WHITE HART

White Hart is one of the most popular pub names throughout England and derives from the insignia of Richard II of 1377. It was a distinctive sign as the hart, a male deer, was known to more people then than it is today. It also became a generic name for pubs.

This White Hart has been here since 1703, when the diarist Samuel Pepys died and Buckingham Palace was first built. It has a long bar with timber beams, an open fire and a wooden sign reading: 'Hop Pickers Wanted, Hard Workers Only'. They have 40 single malt whiskies available.

Chailey

(Map 5 page 9)

Gorse bushes grew aplenty here but when the Saxons moved in they were cleared away for a settlement and it became known as 'Ceacge leah', meaning gorse clearing. On the common there is a fine smock mill. Chailey is said to be the dead centre, from a geographic point of view, of Sussex. It is also the largest parish in the county.

FIVE BELLS

Built in the 1500s, the Five Bells has low beams, open fireplaces and a solid brickwork chimney breast. There is a plaque giving the date of 1600, the time when Shakespeare was at the height of his profession. Originally it was the cottages of three yeomen. In 1783 the Chailey Friendly Society met here, who gave relief to the poor of the village, and they are now the oldest friendly society in Sussex. The inn sign is made of five large metal bells of Sussex wrought iron. It is a fine roadside inn with a tree-covered garden.

HORNS LODGE

Horns Lodge is one of the few pubs left in the county with its own marble ring and they also play several other traditional pub games here. Named after the local hunters, the inn sign carries one gunman impaled on the horns of a stag. It has a flower-filled, Victorian horse water trough outside and there are magnificent views.

KINGS HEAD

The exact site of the dead centre of Sussex is a yew tree at Beards Mill, north-west of the junction at the Kings Head. The Kings Head is a large, old building, described in 1649 as a common victualling house, with what appears to have been a 1920s makeover in Tudor style. In one bar there is a library of books for customers.

Charlton

(Map 1 page 6)

CHARLTON FOX

This building was erected over 500 years ago. It became a pub, the Pig and Whistle, after being used as a bakery. (Since 1681, to go 'pigs and whistle' meant bankruptcy, so the name implied that too many pub visits had had that result.) In 1738 there was a chase by the Charlton Hunt that took over 10 hours to complete and at that time 150 hunters were stabled at Fox Hall, which is the origin of the current name. Occasionally the Fox serves Charlton Hunt Pie, a traditional game pie with a rich sauce. The Women's Institute started here in 1915 and there is a commemorative plaque in the bar.

Chichester

(Map 1 page 6)

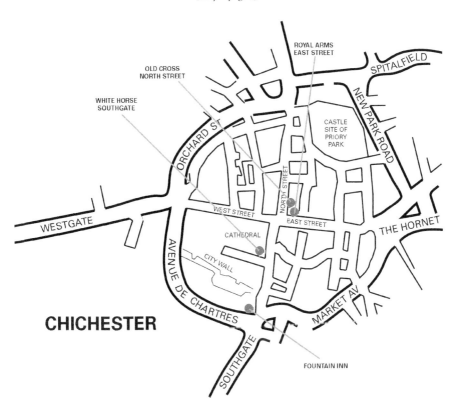

OLD CROSS
NORTH STREET

ROYAL ARMS
EAST STREET

SPITALFIELD

WHITE HORSE
SOUTHGATE

ORCHARD ST

NEW PARK ROAD

CASTLE
SITE OF
PRIORY
PARK

WESTGATE

WEST STREET

NORTH STREET

EAST STREET

THE HORNET

CATHEDRAL

AVENUE DE CHARTRES

CITY WALL

CHICHESTER

MARKET AV

SOUTHGATE

FOUNTAIN INN

Chichester was an old Roman station and its name comes from its original name 'Ceaster' and Cissa's Roman fort, who is mentioned in the *Anglo-Saxon Chronicle* as one of the sons of Aella, first King of the South Saxons. It was recorded in AD 895 as 'Cisseceaster'.

FOUNTAIN INN, Southgate

This town inn was built in the 16th century and is the second oldest in Chichester. The fountain was an heraldic device of the Plumbers' Company and Master Mariners, but the pub name could have come from a nearby spring or well used by

the public. Once owned by the author H.G. Wells and his family, the pub was a meeting place for carriers collecting and delivering locally. Part of the Roman south wall, built in AD 200, runs through the inn

OLD CROSS, North Street
The Old Cross is an historic
inn with Roman foundations.
It is built on the site of a
Roman taverna or dicing
room. On the outside wall
there are two dice around the
word 'Temptation'. It was last
rebuilt in the 1920s when there
was a revival of Tudor-style
buildings. Usually such pubs
were named after a large public
cross and in this case it is a
rather noble one, erected
nearby in 1501.

ROYAL ARMS, East Street
The Royal Arms was
nicknamed 'Ye Olde Punch
Bowl' because of its potent
brew, and Queen Victoria
granted a Royal Charter for
this brew in 1840. Lord
Lumley entertained Elizabeth
I here in 1591. It was once
called the Scarborough Arms
after the Earl of Scarborough
whose private army had
helped Churchill at
Sedgemoor in 1685. It was
rebuilt in 1750, about the
time of the publication of
Grey's *Elegy*, and has
magnificent Italian plasterwork in the Elizabethan
Room.

WHITE HORSE,

South Street

The White Horse is the oldest tavern in the town, dating from 1460 and built during the War of the Roses. It has been a courthouse and was once a Tudor-style building with the second storey overhanging the pavement. There are old oak beams, a stone fireplace and oak settles. The sign of the white horse has been in use since the 15th century, including in the heraldry of the House of Hanover.

Chiddingly

(Map 6 page 9)

This was known as 'Cittingas leah' meaning a clearing in the forest of Citta's people. In the 1830s, the Captain Swing Riots took place and machinery was destroyed here and damage done to farms and churches locally. Over 400 men throughout Sussex were transported to the colonies and 19 were hanged for this. It was once nicknamed Rome because it is on seven hills. Judge Jeffrey's family came from Chiddingly and there is a large family tableau in the church.

SIX BELLS

The pub is an 18th-century hostelry, situated opposite the village church, with a large garden and fishpond. Here there are many artifacts on display including a pianola with rolls of music, stuffed animals, prints and old political cartoons. A huge inglenook fireplace has a seat at each end and there are high-backed settles throughout the pub. On one outside end wall there is an enamel advertisement saying 'Pratts Served Here', but it does not refer to customers. Pratts was a well known petrol company in the 1930s before being absorbed by Esso. One former landlady, at the age of 60, married a man of 26 who eventually inherited the place. On tables are carved the words 'KB 1891', 'The war is over, thank God' and a pejorative reference to another man's fishing abilities. The pub garden is haunted by a big, grey cat. A local woman, who poisoned her husband with an onion pie, was the last female to be hanged publicly in 1856 at Lewes.

Chidham

(Map 1 page 6)

The original Saxons named it 'Ceode ham'. A local farmer found some wild wheat growing here with large ears that he cultivated and thus was born a new strain, which has since been called 'Chidham wheat'.

OLD HOUSE AT HOME

The Old House at Home is named after a Victorian ballad of soldiers dreaming of home from abroad. Many put their pensions into pubs when they returned from wars and named them this. It is three centuries old and is situated in a remote part of Chichester Harbour. The main bar has a heavy beamed ceiling and the walls are brick and plaster with wood, and it has an attractive bar built from brick with a wooden top. They have a secret recipe beer here called 'Old House Bitter' and a special cream of shellfish soup. The area is home to many seabirds and waders.

Chilgrove

(Map 1 page 6)

In Saxon the settlement was known as 'Ceole Graf', meaning gulley grove, and it had become 'Chelegrave' by 1200. Research has shown local hedges are over 1,000 years old and Roman villas have been excavated here.

WHITE HORSE INN

This has been an inn name since the 15th century and and has also been used in the insignia of several City Guilds. A long, two-storey, Sussex house built in the 1750s, it was a stopping place for travellers and traders going to Chichester.

Clayton

(Map 4 page 8)

A large part of the village lies on gault, beds of clay and marl and was known as 'claeg tun' in Saxon, meaning the clay farmstead. This word survives as 'claggy', meaning sticky soil. Norman Hartnell, the Queen's dress designer, is buried in the local churchyard.

JACK AND JILL

Once the Matsfield Arms, the Jack and Jill has been renamed after two windmills nearby. I am grateful to Don Lewry of Newhaven for the following story: His grandfather, a carter, would put a metal shoe under one wheel of a cart coming down the nearby Clayton Hill to slow it down. He would then walk ahead to the shop to buy bacon and eggs and by the time the slowed horse and cart reached him the shoe would be hot enough to cook his breakfast on.

Cocking and Diddling

(Map 1 page 6)

Although the two villages are some distance apart, they form a unit with only one pub between them. Diddling comes from a Saxon group called 'Dyddelingas', meaning Dydel's people, and Cocking, pronounced Kokkun, from 'Coccingas', which meant Cocca's people. The local pond is called Bumblekit and a curious phenomena takes place here called 'foxes brewing', a mist in the trees which forecasts rain.

BLUE BELL INN

The Bluebell Inn is a large, Victorian-style corner pub with several bars. Although this is a fairly common name for pubs, it is not certain if it is named after a real bell painted blue or after the wild flower.

Coleman's Hatch

(Map 5 page 9)

Coleman's Hatch was named after Edmund and Richard Coleman, charcoal burners between 1279 and 1327.

HATCH INN

In the year before Joan of Arc was burned at Rouen, three small cottages were built on this site. Three hundred years later they became a public house called the Cock. Later it became Coleman's Hatch (or gateway) and it led through to the Royal Ashdown Forest. It is only a short distance from Pooh Bridge on Kid's Hill, in the forest. It is noted by the Cyclists' Touring Club as cycle friendly.

Colgate

(Map 3 page 8)

In the highest part of St Leonards Forest, Colgate was connected with the de la Collegate family of 1279. There are many legends about dragons and dragon slayers, a lack of nightingales, snakes and a smuggler, Mick Mills, who ran a race with the Devil gambling his soul and won. Having saved his soul from Hell, he was too wicked for Heaven and as neither wanted him he remains here, wandering around Colgate.

DRAGON

It was here that the last dragon was seen in England, so legend has it. The dragon was used in many coats of arms, particularly by the Tudors. In 1512, as part of Henry VIII's Navy ship programme, the first *Dragon* was built. It is a fine roadside inn with an old-fashioned till and is a noted walkers' pub because of the huge array of sandwiches available.

Compton

(Map 1 page 6)

Compton derives from the Saxon words 'Cumb Tun', meaning valley farmstead, and was known as 'Cumton' by 1015.

COACH AND HORSES

There are two bars at the inn with low ceilings and original beams. It is a delightful 15th-century coaching inn with a white-painted front, and the coaching stables are now an old-fashioned skittle alley. There are only a few genuine village squares left now but Compton has one, nearby.

Cowbeech

(Map 6 page 9)

Cowbeech derives from the word for capped or pollarded trees and in 1261 was known as 'Coppetebeche'.

MERRY HARRIERS

Usually such a pub name denotes either the harrier bird or athletes. The Merry Harriers was a coaching inn built in about 1675, when John Bunyan was writing *Pilgrim's Progress*. It has a beamed ceiling and large, high-back settles. At one time it housed meetings of the Cowbeech Benevolent Institution, established in 1848 for the relief of the sick, and a slate club for members to borrow money.

Crawley

(Map 5 page 9)

Crawley became a new town in 1947 and its name derives from the words 'Crawe Leah' meaning Crow's Wood. It was recorded as 'Crawleia' in 1203.

GEORGE

This was an important coaching inn between London and Brighton. The Prince Regent and his court ate and changed horses here. It opened in 1616, the same year that William Shakespeare died. Outside there is a chilling reminder of the summary justice of the past as the gallows spread from the inn on to the market square. The inn is haunted by Mark Hurston, a former nightwatchman. He can still be heard on patrol. Hurston was noted for delivering wine to residents in their rooms, whether they wanted it or not, and was roundly abused on occasion for waking them. One guest left poison in a bottle and the unfortunate nightwatchman took it away, drank it and died in one of the rooms here.

PUNCH BOWL

The Punch Bowl is an ancient coaching inn on the old main road. The drink 'punch' was introduced to this country during the early 1600s and was a sailor's drink. The word 'punch' comes from the word for number five, panj, in several Indian languages, and the drink was given this name because there were  five ingredients. Originally these were sugar, lemon, brandy, muscatel and roast biscuit.

SHADES

The Shades opened in the 14th century and later holding cells with an underground passageway to the George Hotel were added. Condemned prisoners were led through to be hanged on the wooden structure that is still there. Shades is an old-fashioned word for ghosts, and this pub is haunted by a pipe-smoking man who uses the ladies' lavatory and a woman in grey with a small child. One man went to his room to find the bed on fire, which could not be explained. It was the same room in which the woman and child appear. Landladies have experienced the front door bell ringing at 6am to find no-one there and the bell jammed.

Crowhurst

(Map 7 page 10)

The yew tree at Crowhurst

Crowhurst was first mentioned in AD 771 in a charter of King Offa of Mercia. The manor here was owned by King Harold. In the church-yard there is a yew tree that is 1,000 years old where the Normans hanged a Saxon man because he would not tell the secrets of Harold's treasure.

PLOUGH

Set on a hill overlooking a valley of trees, this is an early Victorian inn with an outside terrace. Although the front has been re-bricked fairly recently, the original tiled roof with dormer windows remains and the side elevation is in the attractive Sussex style.

Cuckfield

(Map 3 page 8)

Cuckfield does not come from cuckoo field, but from 'Cuca's' open space. The writer Andrew Borde was born here in 1490 and wrote the *Merry Tales of the Mad Men of Gotham* that eventually gave rise to Gotham City of Batman and Robin fame. Shakespeare knew of Borde and quoted him in *King John*.

CROWHURST TO DALLINGTON

OCKENDEN MANOR HOTEL

Once a mediaeval manor house with 14 bedrooms, this hotel has a Priests' Hole and enough secret passageways to satisfy anyone. It has been owned by only two families since 1520. A Grey Lady has been seen gliding along the corridors and in the Elizabethan bedroom. Legend has it that she was a chambermaid who died when she was in the tunnel between the old King's Head inn and the hotel in the 19th century. She had been on her way to meet her secret lover.

Dallington

(Map 4 page 8)

In Saxon it was known as 'Dealling tun', meaning the farm of Dealla. Mad Jack Fuller built a 40ft high folly in Dallington, called the Sugar Loaf, in the 19th century. One Dallington man, Timothy Donnelly, fought under General Custer at the Battle of the Little Big Horn in 1876 where he was killed at the age of 18.

SWAN INN

At the same time that Edward III was laying waste Lothian, Scotland, this inn was

built and named the Swan, in 1356, and it refers either to the bird or the royal heraldic insignia. An old inn sign inside the pub is dated 1399. Inside there are bare wooden boards, a fine example of timber-framing left exposed as a room divider, settles and an old church pew. Weatherboarded, tiled and with dormer windows, it has low ceilings throughout and a log-burning fireplace.

Danehill

(Map 5 page 9)

Danehill was recorded as 'Denne' in 1279, meaning a swine pasture, and 'Denhill' in 1437.

RED LION INN

In 1660, at the restoration of Charles II and the reopening of English theatres, this became a stopping point for travellers between London and Lewes. In 1780 the main road was built away from the village. It is timber-framed with plastered walls, and the lounge was once the blacksmith's forge.

Dell Quay

(Map 1 page 6)

In 1280 Dell Quay was known as 'La Delle' and had become 'Dell Key' by 1671. It is close to Apuldram once known as 'apuldor hamm', meaning the apple-tree meadow, which is still noted for fine apple growing.

CROWN AND ANCHOR.

Looking across the harbour, this pub is 500 years old and opened originally for sailors and dockworkers. The quay was built by the Romans and was once a port for overseas trade, but is now a yachting centre. Once ranked as the ninth smallest port in the country, it is now the smallest. The inn has oak beams with open and original fireplaces. There is a

fine, large, curved window overlooking the harbour. One of the first landlords was John Middes. Five revenue men were abducted and held here and allegedly killed in the cellar by smugglers. Later, bodies were found in the garden.

Denton

(Map 6 page 9)

Since AD 801 it has been known as 'Denton', meaning a valley farmstead.

FLYING FISH

This is a unique pub name, formerly the Kicking Donkey, that may derive from seaplanes based at Newhaven during World War One that were nicknamed flying fish. At least 300 years old, it has low ceilings and rough plasterwork with an open fire and an ancient window overlooking the garden. The village church nearby is dedicated to St Leonard, patron saint of sailors in bondage. Occasionally the pub floods inside from an underground spring and outside there is a Victorian pump which fed from this.

Ditchling

(Map 4 page 8)

Ditchling Beacon is the highest point of the South Downs at 813ft. Alfred the Great called it 'Dicelingas', meaning Dicel's people, in AD 850, and it is believed he had a palace nearby.

BULL HOTEL

The Bull has heavy beams and a large, brick inglenook fireplace. The furniture consists of low-back settles and a long refectory table. It is near where the sculptor and designer Eric Gill worked. It was first recorded in 1636 when it was listed in *A Catalogue of Taverns in Tenne Shires* about London, but its history goes back a further 120 years. Staff have frequently seen a full pint slide along a bar and crash on to the ground, although no one was nearby. After this there is a rattling of the door handle as though someone were leaving. Hanging paintings have moved about during the night. When newspapers cost an old five pence each, the village schoolmaster would read out the news to the people here.

WHITE HORSE

Built in the 17th century, the White Horse had secret tunnels, used by smugglers, between it and the church. A male ghost with a propensity for stroking womens' heads has been in residence for many years. Mediums say this is associated with an incident in 1806. Mr Harnott, the landlord, awoke when he heard someone breaking in through a window. He saw two men in the bar, Robert Bignall and John Tingley, and both were criminals. Bignall pulled his pistol. Harnott grabbed him and held him but was shot dead. Following his trial, Bignall was hanged with 3,000 spectators present to watch him swing. They say the ghost is Bignall wandering about in a long cloak. Close by is Wings House, given to Anne of Cleves by Henry VIII and described as The Royal Palace.

Dragons Green

(Map 3 page 8)

Dragons Green is so called because St Leonard's Forest here was the legendary home of dragons.

GEORGE AND DRAGON

Everyone's dream of what a country pub should look like: small and beamed, timber-framed and tile-hung. Here there is a gravestone where the son of a former landlord is buried in the garden. Walter Budd, an albino and epileptic, took his own life after being falsely accused of stealing. It is here where an annual dwile-flonking takes place. This is a game for 12 people dressed in old-fashioned, rural gear. A beer-soaked cloth, the dwile, is put at the end of a pole and thrown at one of the players when the music stops. (Well, that seems to be the idea.) The pub has very low doors and the legend over one reads 'He too proud to bend his head, Takes an aching pate to bed.'

Duncton

(Map 2 page 7)

Duncton is a Saxon village named after the farm of a man called 'Dunnaca'. At the Victorian parish church there is a Dutch bell dated 1369, making it the oldest dated bell in Sussex.

CRICKETERS

An earlier James Dean graces the pub sign at this hostelry, originally opened in the 15th century. He played for Sussex and All England and was landlord in the 19th century. It changed its name in 1860 when it was associated with John Wisden of the cricketers' *Almanac*. This was also the year that bare-knuckle fighting was last legally held in England. During his well documented journey across Sussex, Hilaire Belloc stayed here. There is a skittle alley and portraits of famous cricketers, including James Broadbridge, born 1796, in the bar as well as a large inglenook fireplace and massive chimney.

Eartham

(Map 2 page 7)

The village name translates as earth settlement, spelled 'Urtham' in 1279. The victim of the first railway death came from Eartham. William Huskisson, an MP for Chichester, was killed in 1830 at the opening of the Manchester to Liverpool railway.

GEORGE

The George is 17th-century and has a stone-flagged public bar. Originally, pubs called the George referred to Saint George, patron saint of England, but since 1714 there have been six King Georges and usually the inn sign says which one it refers to. The poet William Hayley lived at nearby Eartham House and although he was offered the position of Poet Laureate he turned it down.

Eastbourne

(Map 6 page 9)

From Old English 'burna', meaning stream, Eastbourne was recorded in the Domesday Book as 'Burna Estbuan'.

BEACHY HEAD

Beachy Head is an isolated inn on the downs near where so many suicides have taken place. In 1690 the Battle of Beachy Head took place here, and the combined fleet of English and Dutch navies took on the French fleet. The first lighthouse was built off the head in 1828, constructed of wood. This was replaced with a stronger building six years later. Before the lighthouse was erected, the Revd Jonathon Darby hollowed out a cave above high-tide level and put a lantern outside so sailors could escape from wrecked ships. Near this pub there are the remains of a bronze age settlement. The name comes from the French 'beau chef' and it was also known as the Devil's Cape because of the number of boats foundering here.

LAMB

Some parts of this pub date back over 700 years and it is one the oldest buildings in Eastbourne. It was well used by smugglers and other criminals in the past. The remains of a Roman boat were found nearby during redevelopment. The town was known as 'The Empress of Watering Holes' in Victorian times. An underground passage once connected the pub to the old parsonage.

The low-beamed main bar was once a ballroom and the chairs came from the German Embassy in London. In 1852 Dr Darling was giving a talk on spiritualism at the Lamb during which there was a most dreadful clap of thunder and his audience ran out on him.

East Dean

(Map 6 page 9)

East Dean was known as 'Estdena', meaning east valley, in 1150. Nearby Birling Gap was perfect for smuggling and wreckers brought boats ashore with false lights. In the late 1800s the first cable office was built to provide electrical communication to the Continent by underwater cable. Crowling, a local house, was noted in the 1800s for gin smuggling. This became the home of Edith Nesbitt, author of *The Railway Children*. Nearby, Friston Pond was the first village pond to be listed as an ancient monument.

TIGER INN

In the early 19th century tiger was the name for a boy-groom dressed in livery of black and yellow. Small, negro boys were most fashionable at the time. It is also an heraldic device used by Sir Francis Walsingham. Originally built in the late 1200s, the pub is made from flint and has the original oak beams. It is built on a village green amid pretty cottages and has low ceilings, a large stone fireplace and is decorated with many artefacts, including two tigers' heads and animal horns. Part of the green and houses were used by local militia during the Napoleonic Wars.

Eastergate

(Map 2 page 7)

In the 13th century the village was known as Eastern Gate. The murals on the village hall here were painted by Byam Shaw and include St Wilfrid landing at Selsey, King Harold hunting wild boar, Elizabeth I at a deer hunt in 1592 and the flight of Charles II through Sussex. In the church there is a rare piece of mediaeval stained glass, a coat of arms, from 1360.

WILKES HEAD

The Wilkes Head is named after Sir John Wilkes, a politician who was notorious in the days of George III. He was a Whig expelled from Parliament and ended up in the Tower of London for attacking the government in 'North Briton'. Wilkes was a member of the infamous Hellfire Club and co-rake Lord Sandwich told him, 'You will either die on the gallows or die of the pox' to which Wilkes replied, 'It depends, my lord, on whether I embrace your principles or your mistress'. The building dates from 1746 and was licensed in 1803, just two years before the Battle of Trafalgar, and has an original inglenook fireplace and oak beams.

East Grinstead

(Map 5 page 9)

The town has a market charter from 1221 and was known as 'Green stede', meaning verdant growth.

DORSET ARMS

This was once known as the New Inn, then the Cat as a 16th-century inn and, once, as the Ounce. More recently, it was renamed after Thomas Sackville, Earl of Dorset and a local benefactor. In 1910 the World Boxing Championship, between John Cribb and Molyneux, was held in East Grinstead, and the town was over-run by thousands of people. Here they charged £3 a night; about two weeks wages for working people. Details of this pugilistic meeting are on the walls of this inn.

East Hoathly

(Map 6 page 9)

East Hoathly derives from the Saxon 'haed leah', meaning a clearing on the heathland. A steam train was named after the village in 1898. In 1810 Henry Rich set up business here making Sussex trugs and presented one to Queen Victoria in 1851.

FORESTERS ARMS

Once this area was noted for forestry and woodworking industries, and the pub takes it name from that. It is a three centuries old, simple, beamed building, divided into a public bar and saloon, and has steps leading up to the entrance. One bar ceiling is covered with sheet music from the 1940s and 1950s and there is an art deco cello cover and a wooden fork and paddle from  the maltings in it. It was on the main Eastbourne to London coach run.

KING'S HEAD

The pub was called Burges after one landlord, then the Maypole and finally the King's Head. It is a large ivy-covered village centre pub and is noted for raising money for charity. Built in the late 17th century, local diarist Thomas Turner lived here as pub owner in the 1700s and kept a very detailed diary. Turner is buried in the local churchyard where there is also a

Norman pillar piscine and an altar piece designed by William Morris. In 1761 there was a cockfight arranged here between the Gentlemen of Hoathly and Pevensey with prizes of 10 guineas.

East Lavant

(Map 1 page 6)

ROYAL OAK

Here at the Royal Oak the London stagecoaches changed horses. It has oak beams, open fireplaces and horse brasses. Two smugglers murdered a revenue man here 200 years ago during a gunfight. They were tried for their wickedness and eventually dispatched to meet their maker, but one of them never made it. Since then a tall, thin and bearded man has been seen wandering around the pub, mainly in the bedrooms. At the inn there is a grandfather clock. The children of a previous landlord tinkered with this clock and were later visited by things in the night and the clock chimed at uneven times. They saw a small man with a full beard and old-fashioned clothing coming into their room and smiling at them.

Elsted

(Map 1 page 6)

Two explanations have been given for the name Elsted: either it comes from 'elna stede', meaning the place of elder trees, or from Aella, first king of the South Saxons in about AD 480.

THREE HORSESHOES

Originally built over 300 years ago for cattle drivers and travellers, it has three bars with oak beams, terracotta floors and an inglenook fireplace. Poet Hilaire Belloc used this pub when he and three friends walked from Robertsbridge to South Harting in 1902, recorded in *The Four Men*.

Three horseshoes was the heraldry of the Worshipful Company of Farriers (1673) and the Ferrers, earls of Derby.

Faygate

(Map 3 page 8)

In Saxon this was known as 'Feo hege', a hedged enclosure for cattle, and became Fay Gate by 1614, the same year that Pocahontas married John Rolfe in Virginia.

CHERRY TREE

The Cherry Tree is a traditional, timber-framed pub that was once a coaching inn. Built in 1660, during the Restoration of Charles II, it has ancient beams and an inglenook fireplace. Not long ago a parish council suggested that there should be a town sign showing fairies sitting on a gate because the town was originally known as Fey-gate. Sweet, perhaps, but the Saxon name is the more likely origin. In 1614 a Faygate widow claimed to have seen a dragon and her story was published. She described it as having a nine-foot long body with black and red scales and said, 'It was very proud and arrogant with incipient wings'. At the Holmbush Inn nearby there is a yellow and black road sign from the early days of motoring; most of these were taken down during World War Two to confuse the Germans if they landed.

Fernhurst

(Map 1 page 6)

Recorded as 'Fernherst' in the 13th century, meaning a fern covered hill, it is pronounced Farnest. The Fabian Society, George Bernard Shaw and the Webbs lived in Friday's Hill House nearby. In the 19th century a Fernhurst man got married and told the vicar, 'I ain't got no money you know. Y'must take it out in taties'.

KING'S ARMS

The King's Arms has been a roadside inn since the late 1600s, is built in Sussex sandstone and tile and has log burning fires in an L-shaped bar. A nearby barn has been turned into the King's Barn for functions. The pub is in open farmland with camping facilities behind it. A huge foundry cast cannons here as late as 1770.

RED LION

This is another Red Lion, one of the most popular pub names. Opened in 1592 as an alehouse, in 1621 landlord William Fynche went before the bishop for 'selling ale during praying time'. A later landlord, Robert Purse, was given the inn for a peppercorn rent for 1,000 years in 1699. It is a village inn, in red brick and tile, on the green with rustic furniture outside.

Findon

(Map 4 page 8)

The name derives from either the Saxon 'fin dun', meaning woodheap hill, or 'fina dun', meaning woodpecker hill. A Roman well, 200ft deep, was discovered here many years ago containing farm animal bones.

GUN INN

Situated near Cissbury Ring, the Gun was rebuilt in 1675, when the Royal Observatory at Greenwich was founded by Charles II. Many of the old beams came from sailing ships. It was named after the shotgun rather than an artillery gun as sporting folk used to leave their fowling pieces outside when lunching. In a Rabelaisian contest some years ago, a local woman took on 15 men in a beer-drinking competition and swallowed her pint in 4.4 seconds.

VILLAGE HOUSE HOTEL

The Village House Hotel was built in 1527, when Henry VIII and Francis I of France formed an alliance. The inn houses racing silks from nearby stables and was once a magistrates' court. Having decided upon the guilt of criminals, they were taken

straight round to the village green and dispatched to meet their maker. Because it was on a main route through Sussex, here foregathered a large number of rascals, highwaymen and footpads, and the hangman was kept busy. Each year in September the Findon sheep fair is held, as it has been for seven centuries.

Fittleworth

(Map 2 page 7)

The village was known as 'Fitela's Woro', a Saxon enclosure owned by 'Fitela'. There is said to be buried treasure in a wood close by, guarded by a spirit dressed in brown who appears if anyone approaches the site. Edward Elgar lived nearby for several years and composed his cello concerto and chamber music here.

SWAN

The Swan is a popular name for a pub, adopted because it was the emblem of innocence. Behind the pub is an old millhouse and stream. Landscape painter John Constable stayed at this four centuries old inn. A curious feature is a former inn sign that showed a naked woman riding a swan, which was once considered rude. Lore has it that because she looked like Queen Victoria the then landlord was obliged to paint clothes over her. Some years ago this sign was stolen and reappeared in an auction at Haslemere, but it was promptly returned. A collection of coshes, shillelaghs and policemens' truncheons hang in the bar.

Fletchling

(Map 5 page 9)

Fletchling is a Saxon settlement whose name comes from 'Fleccingas', meaning Flecca's people. In the 15th century, the villagers were major producers of bows and arrows for the Battle of Agincourt. Edward Gibbon, author of *The Decline and Fall of the Roman Empire*, was buried here in 1794.

GRIFFIN

This pub is 400 years old and an old coaching inn in the village centre. The griffin was a fabulous monster, the offspring of the lion and the eagle, king of birds. On the tall chimney there are marks where locals sharpened their sickles and knives. It has a collection of old pews and wheel-backed chairs. The village was home to the Bonfire Boys whose behaviour was so bad that they eventually had to be stopped by the authorities. After the Battle of Lewes in 1264, many knights were buried at the local church still in their armour.

ROSE AND CROWN

The Rose and Crown is a brick-built, tile-hung, 16th-century pub with dormer

windows and a stone inglenook fireplace. The original building dates from 1150, the time of King Stephen. It has Norman wattle and daub remains found on a wall in 1939, now preserved in a glass-fronted case. It is very low beamed with original horse brasses. The Rose also has deep marks near the fireplace where local people sharpened their knives and sickles.

Frant

(Map 5 page 9)

Once called 'Fearnibja', meaning the place of ferns, Frant had 20 ironworks in 1600. One document from AD 956 describes it as 'Fyrnban'. Three Frant men were with Jack Cade in the 1450 rebellion, and in 1793 18 soldiers died from smallpox and were buried in Frant churchyard. It was a smuggling centre and affected by the Swing Riots of 1830. Richard Budgen, born in Frant in 1680, made a large scale map of Sussex showing all roads in 1724.

ABERGAVENNY ARMS

For many years pubs were used as magistrates' and coroner's courts as they were central in villages and small towns. This pub is originally 15th-century and was used in the 18th century for trying local offences. The cellars were used to lock up prisoners. At least five men were hanged on the village green outside the pub for stealing sheep. Some of the beams came from a ship that sailed in the Spanish Armada in 1588.

Fulking

(Map 4 page 8)

Originally a Saxon farm known as 'Folca's tun', the settlement became known as 'Fochintone' by 1086. Outside the pub there is a fresh water spring once used for watering sheep and, even in summertime, the water is bitterly cold.

SHEPHERD AND DOG

An absolute treasure once used by sheep drovers going to local sheep fairs and markets. It nestles below the South Downs and was built over 600 years ago. Inside

the pub, bucolic ephemera, including shepherds' crooks, abound. Every area in the country had their own way of counting sheep, and in Sussex shepherds counted the sheep in pairs: wuntherum, twotherum, cockerum, cutherum, sheterum, shaterum, wineberrry, wigtail, tarry-diddle, den, with each word counting two sheep. John Ruskin, art critic and historian, was a regular visitor and helped organise the first pumphouse to gather spring water. The upstairs of the pub is haunted by a former landlord, Mr Liquorice, and the downstairs, by noisy poltergeists.

Glynde

(Map 6 page 9)

It was recorded in 1279 as Burne Juxta Glynde. Glynde Place was built in the 1200s, and in 1479 the current version of the building was erected. Glynde was the home of the pink-faced Southdown sheep that have been bred here since the 1700s, originally by John Ellman who is buried in the churchyard. Ellman, an early socialist, gave houses to his workers when they married. In 1934 John Christie, whose family had lived at Glyndebourne since 1617, opened Glyndebourne Opera.

TREVOR ARMS

The Trevor Arms is well known to visitors to the opera, is close to Mount Caburn and was named after the Trevor family. Mount Cabourn is a large chalk outcrop,

occupied in the Iron Age, where fortifications were built, and is one of the higher landmarks in Sussex at 480ft above sea level. On the downs, some unusual footprints have been seen said to be left by witches dancing at midnight. The sun moves in a clockwise manner in the Northern hemisphere and because of this people always dance clockwise or sun-wise. To dance the other way was considered evil and witches danced this way on their sabbaths to please the devil. This was called 'dancing widdershins'. There are three bars, one with a view of the hills.

Goring by Sea

(Map 2 page 7)

Goring by Sea comes from 'Garinges', meaning the place of Gora's people, and it was known as Goryng by the 13th century.

BULL INN

The Bull is an old smuggling inn, built 500 years ago, situated near the village cricket green. A veritable warren of panelled bars, it has a large inglenook fireplace and brass cooking equipment displayed. Old photographs of the village and steam engines hang in the bars and it is a fine roadside inn.

Graffham
(Map 2 page 7)

Early bronze age remains exist here, and in Saxon times it was called 'graf ham', meaning a settlement by a grove of trees. In 1807 a highwayman called 'Alien' took refuge here while being chased by the militia. He hid near Graffam Pond and killed at least one soldier with his pistol before he was shot dead. Frequently, 'Alien' makes an appearance around the pond dressed in a long cloak and tricorne hat.

FORESTERS ARMS

Built in 1609, as Bermuda was first settled by the British, the pub was first called the Star and Garter and later renamed after the meeting place of the local free foresters. It is situated just off the South Downs Way.

Hailsham
(Map 6 page 9)

The name comes from the Saxon words 'Haegels Ham', meaning the home of Haegel. There were 17 salt workings nearby but they were badly affected by the Norman invasion. In 1252 Henry III granted market rights, which was stopped in 1639 and restarted again in the 1700s. In 1780 rope making was started by Thomas Burfield and included making ropes for execution.

GRENADIER HOTEL

Opened in the 1800s during the Napoleonic Wars, the pub was originally called the British Grenadier. These were soldiers who threw the grenades and, at one time, it was used to describe the tallest and best men in any regiment. Now it is only applied

to the Grenadier Guards. In 1811 most soldiers had left the area and the landlord resorted to buying and selling owls for a living. It has been run by the same family for half a century. Inside the pub, there is an old gas lamp and it is situated near the Cuckoo Trail. They run a 'Milk and Ale' club to raise money for charity and in 10 years have collected £90,000 for Guide Dogs for the Blind.

CORN EXCHANGE

It is the oldest inn in Hailsham, dating from the 1400s, and has original panelling and lots of brass and copper on display. Until recently it was called the Crown. It was once a staging post in coaching days. It was the headquarters of the Prosecuting Society, a group of gentlemen who put up rewards locally for the arrest of criminals, and it was also a courtroom where they were tried.

Halfway Bridge

(Map 2 page 7)

HALFWAY BRIDGE INN

In the early 1700s it was a staging post for coaches changing horses. Recently an old bricked-up cellar was cleared out to create extra space, but it seems to have released an old apparition said to look like a highwayman or stagecoach driver. There is an old fireplace and period furniture is used in the bars. Nearby is Ell Bridge on the River Lod where locals used to catch eels and elvers.

Hartfield

(Map 5 page 9)

Once roamed by harts and deer, the Saxons called the settlement 'Heorot feld'. In 1905 the Milne family arrived at Hartfield and bought Cotchford Farm. A small bridge was built over the river in 1907, now known as Pooh

Sticks bridge. In the 1920s, A.A. Milne wrote the Winnie-the-Pooh stories. Young Milne visited the shops here with his nanny, Olive Brockwell, who became Alice in the stories. She is buried at Guestling.

ANCHOR INN

It was built during the reign of Edward IV, in 1465, as a thatched-roof farmhouse and became a pub in 1745. There is a list of owners going back to that date, the same year as the first recorded women's cricket match at Surrey and the first performance of *God Save the King* at Drury Lane. The building was once used as a women's workhouse and the ankle chains that were used to control them are displayed in the bar. The invention of iron anchors by Anacharis the Greek to secure boats dates from 600 BC. Prior to this, large stones had been used for this purpose. Years ago, a rich man disguised as a tramp wandered around Sussex to find the kindest villagers. The people of Hartfield were the most generous to him and so he left money for the Hartfield Good Friday Dole.

GALLIPOT INN,

Galleypot Street

The building is over 400 years old and was once a row of cottages. Gallipots were small pots used for medicines, brought in by galleys from the Mediterranean, and it is also the nickname for an apothecary. Originally, the cottages were owned by three brothers. One, brother, Albert Sands, was a potter and made gallipots for the trade and another, William, brewed

beer and named the pub Gallipot when he licensed it. He was granted a beer licence for 2s 6d by the Excise Officer. There is a mini-farm of ducks, rabbits and guinea pigs and spectacular views over the downs. They still keep some gallipots at the pub.

Hastings

(Map 7 page 10)

The town was first recorded as 'Haestingas' in AD 790, named after a Danish war lord, Haesta. Here William the Conqueror mustered his army prior to the battle at Senlac (lake of blood) in 1066. Hastings was an original Cinque Port that received special privileges for supplying men and ships to the king.

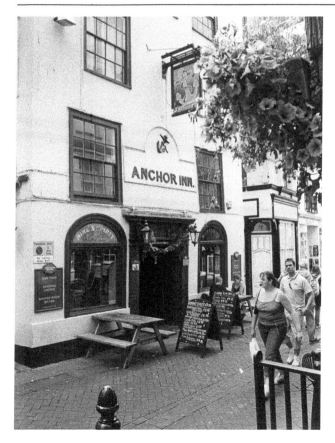

ANCHOR INN,

George Street

The Anchor Inn is one of the oldest pubs in the Hastings old town. Built opposite the beach, it was once a haven for smugglers and there used to be a maze of tunnels between all the local pubs. It is over 400 years old and has low beams. Now the town ghost tour starts here with the tale of a man who was hanged in the back bar and who has been seen on many occasions.

CINQUE PORTS ARMS, All Saints Street

Hastings has been a Cinque Port since the days of Edward the Confessor and this attractive town pub is named after that occasion. The Cinque ports are Hastings, Dover, Romney, Hythe and Sandwich. Through silting up over the years, the only two left as ports are Hastings and Dover. Near this inn is the birthplace of Sir Cloudesley Shovel, Admiral of the Fleet in 1707. The inn was known as the Chequer in 1642 when owned by Richard Tester and first became known as the Cinque Ports in 1824.

KING'S HEAD, Courthouse Street

Situated in the Old Town, the King's Head is haunted by a woman who hangs around outside the ladies' lavatory. She is dressed as a young scullery maid wearing a mob cap and appears to be terrified. Over 200 years ago the kitchen staff and maids lived in the cellar of the pub, which was later rebuilt to become the toilets. According to old records, a scullery maid was savagely beaten by her employer and managed to crawl back to her bed where she died.

QUEEN ADELAIDE, West Street

Located in a side street off the front, this is a most delightful old-fashioned pub with 200 whisky jugs hanging from the ceiling and a ship's figurehead on display. It is possible that John Logie Baird drank here when he was living at nearby Lindon Crescent inventing the television. Queen Adelaide married the third son of George III in 1804, and he became William IV in 1830. This is another must see pub before it is modernised.

ROYAL STANDARD, East Street

The royal standard has changed with history. Edward III introduced the fleur de lys of France and James I the Scottish lion with the Irish harp. The present royal standard dates from the accession of Queen Victoria, but the Hastings pub carries the standard of King Harold. This corner pub is said to have been haunted by a mermaid, many years ago, with mournful eyes peering in through a window.

STAG, All Saints Street

There is a collection of mummified cats at this old smugglers' inn and an old sea captain is still in residence, often seen sitting in the bar. The cats belonged to a local witch, Hannah Clarke, and were bricked up alive as a cure against the plague of 1665. The pub also has its own game called 'Loggitts'. The ghost of Thomas Becket, the murdered Archbishop, has been seen in the town, and an organ has been heard playing from an empty church. Cries, groans and clinking of chains have been heard from dungeons built for prisoners, and on certain days a mirage of Hastings Castle can be seen out at sea as it would have appeared centuries ago. In the ninth century a cock woke up the occupying Danes as the locals were about to attack them. In recognition of this, the townspeople invented a game called cock-in-the-pot where sticks and stones were thrown at a pot holding a cockerel and whoever broke it got the bird.

YE OLD PUMPHOUSE,
George Street

The pub is just off the beach in one of the oldest streets in Hastings. It is a Tudor-style hostelry with log fires. Once a town pumphouse was on the site, and the original building was built in the 14th century. It is cris-crossed inside and out with old beams. The furniture is deep crimson and there are even four-poster beds. As one would expect in an old port, Old Tom's Tattoo parlour is next door.

Haywards Heath

(Map 3 page 8)

STAR

The Star is an early Victorian inn with wooden panelling and three separate bars in one room. There are some original snob windows and hunting pictures over the bar. The term snob comes from the registering system at Eton College. Boys

not from aristocracy were registered as *sine nobilitas*, without nobility, which was abbreviated to sn.ob. The star was originally a religious reference to the Virgin Mary, one of whose titles was 'Star of the Sea' (Stella Maris) and, since 1634, has appeared on the arms of the Worshipful Company of Innholders.

Heathfield

(Map 5 page 9)

Heathfield meant open land covered in heather, and, in 1234, the town was recorded as 'Hadfeld'. Once Heathfield had a natural gas supply, providing sufficient gas locally each day until the 1930s.

CROSS IN HAND

At over 450 years old, the Cross in Hand is an historic pub. Crusaders, three centuries before the pub was built, met up here before embarking from Rye to France and thence to the Holy Land to fight the Saracens. The first thing villagers would see as the Crusaders marched would be the Holy Cross, which was carried ahead of the troops.

On 14 April each year, until the last century, there was a local fair day at Heathfield. An old woman was said to appear there and turn loose the first cuckoo of spring from her basket and then turn over your money for luck. At one time, the landlord of this pub prepared a feast of roast beef and plum puddings for the two fairs held annually.

STAR INN

Pilgrims used this pub in the 14th century and it is located next to the parish church. It has low ceilings with exposed beams, an inglenook fireplace and copper and brass ornaments. Records show it as being here in 1348 to lodge and feed the masons of the church and later show it was used as a coaching inn between Winchester and Canterbury.

The church gave its blessing to the inn and called it the Starre. In 1606 the Revd Robert Hunt, Vicar of Old Heathfield, and six men from the Star went to North America. He became the first Anglican clergyman to settle there, and there is a plaque to commemorate this venture at the pub.

Hellingly

(Map 6 page 9)

The name derives from the Saxon 'Hlellnga leah', meaning settlers on a tongue of land. The village contains the only known Celtic ciric in Sussex and part of the church, started in 1190, is built into it. The ciric was a burial ground raised above ground level to keep the dead dry and is the Celtic symbol of immortality.

BOSHIP FARM HOTEL

This pub was once a farmhouse, built about 1652. There is an exotic ghost here who tucks people up in bed and then kisses them. This has been reported by both guests and staff at the hotel. One woman working there said she had just gone to bed and her bedclothes were over the lower part of her face. They were then pulled down underneath her chin and she felt arms around her and a light kiss on the face. These reports go back to the 1940s but there is no known story behind them.

Henley

(Map 1 page 6)

At the time of Charles I, Henley was known as 'Hounley', and originally in Saxon as 'hund leah', meaning a clearing where hunting hounds were kept.

DUKE OF CUMBERLAND

This pub was built in the late 1400s and has old beams, panelling, open fires and a tiny quarry-tiled public bar. The first landlord was recorded in 1726. Outside there are large, furnished gardens with spring-fed trout pools. A fishing net stands outside the kitchen and whenever fish are needed for the table they are scooped out. A meandering, stone path leads through terraces and bushes to the front door, which has a cobbled terrace. This is another 'must' as such places are disappearing.

Herstmonceux

(Map 6 page 9)

The name Herstmonceux came from the Monceux family and Herst Castle, which was built in the 15th century by Sir Roger de Fiennes. The village is famous for Sussex 'trugs' from the Saxon word 'trog', meaning a basket made from chestnut and willow, which were first displayed nationally at the Great Exhibition of 1851.

BREWERS ARMS

The Brewers Company was granted arms in the 15th century and this pub name

reflects this occasion. The inn sign is usually three barrels with three pairs of crossed sheaves of corn on it. The building used to be a row of cottages in the 17th century and was first recorded as a 'beer shop' in 1841, when the first edition of *Punch* was published. It is tile-hung with brick and weatherboarding, two beamed bars and a collection of antiques and grandfather clocks.

WOOLPACK INN

In 1583, as Newfoundland was annexed by Britain, this building opened as Marlings, a private house, and became a cider and alehouse in 1724. In 1732 the first landlord died and left his 'cyder press' to his servant, Judith Stedwell, and his iron mortar and pestle to Samuel Pocock. By 1838 it was known as the Woolpack Inn. In 1924 at a Herstmonceux WI meeting the pub landlady, Elizabeth Angear, helped with a demonstration of chocolate making. She then started making home-dipped chocolates at the pub, which led to a large Sussex sweet making business.

Heyshott

(Map 1 page 6)

There have been settlements in this area for almost 4,000 years and in Saxon times the settlement was known as 'haeo sceat', meaning land overgrown with heather. Richard Cobden, a founder of Free Trade and battler against the Victorian corn laws, was born here.

UNICORN

This is a legendary animal said to have the body of a horse and one horn on its forehead. This horn, in mythology, had magic powers. Unicorn was also the name of a Scottish gold coin in the 15th and 16th centuries. It was on the arms of the Worshipful Company of Waxmakers, the Worshipful Company of Goldsmiths and the Worshipful Society of Apothecaries. This pub was once a cottage but in 1843 it became an L-shaped inn with a large inglenook fireplace and built-in seats.

High Hurstwood

(Map 5 page 9)

MAYPOLE

The pub was built in 1871, when the Tichborne Claimant (Arthur Orton) began his claim for the Tichborne inheritance and Stanley and Livingston met, and was formerly a coaching inn. The building first went up as a timber-framed farmhouse in the 15th century. Most pubs named this were located near maypoles where local children danced on May Day, but its origins go back to pagan times. In 1583 Philip Stubbes said of the maypole, 'the Maie pole is a stinking idol around which God-fearing people would dance as heathens' and in 1644 they were banned, along with Christmas, by the Commonwealth Parliament. The pub has an L-shaped bar and a large garden.

Hooe
(Map 6 page 9)

Hooe derives from the Saxon 'Hoh', meaning a spur of land, and south of the village is the site of an abandoned Saxon village, Northeye. There is a Saxon coffin lid in the local church.

LAMB INN

A curious rule was created by the Abbot of Bexhill when granting a licence for this pub: from Christmas to May the fire had to be kept going, day and night, and the pub kept open so shepherds could bring their lambs in and keep them warm during the lambing season. Dating from 1520, it had a reputation for smugglers and their battles with the Revenue men. An earlier landlord, Bill Trubshawe, was a friend of the actor David Niven. Niven had erected a road-side sign here which read, 'TRUBSHAWE HAS A LITTLE LAMB, 12 MILES'.

RED LION

Built over five centuries ago when smuggling and general wickednesses were rife, the Red Lion was used as a headquarters for criminals. In the 18th century the

Groombridge gang were the local rascals and the landlord of this pub, James Blackman, was a leading member. Six lime trees were planted outside to tell the smugglers it was a 'safe' pub and the trees are still there now. The smugglers used this pub to grind tobacco and snuff, and every now and again the sound of heavy boots can be heard walking about and there is the smell of snuff in the air.

Hooksway

(Map 1 page 6)

ROYAL OAK

One couple, Alfred and Carrie Ainger, ran this pub for 64 years, up to the 1970s. There are photographs and newspaper cuttings about them in the bar. When a licensing board queried Mr Ainger about sanitary arrangements he said, 'But sir, I have nine acres of field'. The old four-ale bar, four centuries old, has a brick floor. Charles II, King Alphonse of Spain and Edward VII used this inn on local hunting trips. Nearby is Telegraph House, part of a chain signal system of naval semaphore stations from Portsmouth to Admiralty Arch, London. It took 19 minutes for the news to arrive in London when Nelson's body arrived in Portsmouth in 1805.

Horam

(Map 6 page 9)

In AD 950 this village was known as 'Horham', which meant a dirty settlement in Saxon and was probably named so because of the muddy conditions after heavy rains.

GUN INN

Years ago, the local quarries produced iron that was then manufactured into guns, and nearby Chiddingly was known as the iron hammer. Built in 1450, when Cade's rebellion was defeated by Royal troops, the Gun was first licensed as an inn in 1619 and later as a coaching inn, and was named after the large guns produced here. The inn was extended and the original small kitchen was built into the main structure. Both floor areas are made from red brick. There is a collection of hunting horns and a most extraordinary pair of large, black clogs.

Horsham

(Map 3 page 8)

In *Reminiscences of Horsham* Harry Burton reports several cases of wife sales here in the 19th century. Mrs Smart was sold in 1820 for three shillings and sixpence and went to live at Billingshurst with Mr Greenfield. At the November Fair, in 1825, a journeyman blacksmith put his wife up for sale here along with one of his three children and sold them for £2 5s. The last reported case of wife selling was in 1844 when Ann Holland (known as Pin-toe Annie) was sold for £1 10s. Led into the market place with a halter round her neck, she was sold to Mr Johnson. Horsham used to be an Assizes town, and it was here that the last man was pressed to death for burglary and murder in 1844. Nearby Doomsday Green was named after George Doomsday, a farmer in 1650.

BEAR

Next door to the imposing town hall, the pub building dates back to the 12th century. The bear is found on the insignia of several noble families and when

connected with an heraldic device is usually the Brown or Black Bear. In this case, the bear refers to the bear baiting that went on outside this pub until it was banned in 1835. The bar has wooden panelling and a large number of bear artifacts. At the side of the bar is a hidden door and it is haunted by three ghosts.

DOG AND BACON

The name is a corruption of the Dorking Beacon that can be seen, on a clear day, from the pub. It is a fine roadside inn surrounded by large trees on an old green, and there are 18th-century weatherboarded houses nearby.

GREEN DRAGON

The curious name comes from the coat of arms of the earls of Pembroke and the fact that most dragons appear green. This is a six centuries old building with wattle and daub walls and an inglenook fireplace with a seat at each end. It has huge oak beams and intimate booths in the brick and plaster bars. Outside there are attractive, modern rock and water features. Once it was the administrative centre for the Lord of the Manor, and there is a central well here that provided water for the brewery.

YE OLDE KINGS HEAD

Dating from 1410, although much modernised, it is three storeys tall and situated in the town centre. The head on the inn sign is that of Henry VIII. It has Tudor-style décor and original 12th century vaults. Next door there is an old Inland Revenue

office. This was opened specially, between 1855 and 1881, because of the amount of financial transactions made in the town. The first manager was called Mr Thrift.

Houghton

(Map 2 page 7)

One of the oldest place names in Sussex, Houghton was recorded as 'Hohtun' in AD 683, meaning a farmstead on a spur of land. In 1791 two local women,

Big Ben and Mendoza, took part in a bare-fist, prize fight here, won by Big Ben. A beerhouse, owned by Nancy Green, was situated at a nearby hamlet next door to the village pound for stray animals. Here 'beer was sold by the pound', a joke in weights and measures.

GEORGE AND DRAGON

This is an attractive building made from flint and stone with an exceedingly small front door. Built in 1200, it gave refuge to King Charles II when he was on the run after the Battle of Worcester in 1651. A plaque on the small door announces this. It was used by Hilaire Belloc on his travels through Sussex, and he described it as a 'small and revered inn'. Smugglers also used it and there were secret tunnels there for bringing in contraband.

Hove

(Map 4 page 8)

Hove comes from the Old English word 'Hufe' or hood, meaning a place of shelter, and it was recorded in 1288 as 'La Huuve'.

BOW STREET RUNNER

In 1806 eight officers were taken on by Bow Street Court, London, to investigate serious crimes, and they became the world's first detective force. This small pub is named after them. They were later named Peelers as they were under the command of Sir Robert Peel. Many years later, police had blue lamps erected outside every police station except one. That was at Bow Street because Queen Victoria passed it on her way to the opera and said the lamp reminded her of the blue room where her husband had died, so they had to have a white lamp.

HANGLETON MANOR

This is the oldest non-church building in Hove and was erected by Richard Bellingham, Sheriff of Sussex, between 1543 and 1553. It has 16th-century panelling and floor tiles, a Tudor heraldic ceiling and a Jacobean fireplace. A dovecote in the grounds was cursed by a monk who hated the bird droppings from it, and it is now haunted by phantom pigeons. Stories abound of trampings of boots in the long gallery and sounds of heavy balls being rolled as there used to be an Elizabethan skittle alley.

Hunston

(Map 1 page 6)

The village name has hardly changed in almost 1,000 years and was originally known as 'Hunestan', meaning Huna's Stone.

SPOTTED COW

Often this pub name refers to the nursery rhyme, 'Hey diddle diddle, The cat and the fiddle, The cow jumped over the moon'. Built in the 16th century as a farmhouse, it

became an inn during the 17th century. It is a fine roadside inn with a pleasant garden and is half slate-fronted. The pub name is unusual but there is another one at Angmering.

Hurstpierpoint

(Map 4 page 8)

Hurstpierpoint is known locally as 'Hurst'. The clergyman writer Revd Sabine Baring-Gould lived here. Nanny Smart, an 18th-century witch, lived here and said she would not die until somebody bought her secrets. A Cuckfield man bought them for a halfpenny and she died in a blue flame.

NEW INN

An exotic phantom has taken up residence here and leaves the aroma of a good cigar in the cellars. It can be naughty at times; glasses and bottles have leapt from shelves and once a leather strip of horse brasses came away from a hook landing several feet away on a table. While out in the garden, one landlord heard a large crash and rushed in to find an ashtray had broken into eight equal triangles of glass. This happened again two weeks later but is still without explanation.

Icklesham

(Map 7 page 10)

The name derives from 'Icel Hamm', meaning a Saxon's home, and in an eighth-century Royal Charter it had become Iklesham.

QUEEN'S HEAD

An old man has been seen sitting by a fireplace here. He is dressed like a shepherd or farm worker in an old pull-down hat and is chewing straw. It is said to be Mr Gutsell, a former landlord, who died here in the 19th century. Built in 1632 and converted into an alehouse in the early 1830s, it is a

timber-framed building with the name on the roof, which can be seen from many miles away. The fine, tessellated inn sign shows the late Queen Mother as Warden of the Cinque Ports.

Iden

(Map 7 page 10)

A pretty village now, Iden was once called 'denn', which meant swine pasture with yew trees.

BELL INN

At almost 1,000 years old, it was here when the Norman Conquest started and was run by monks for pilgrims. There are two ghosts here. One has been seen in the gentlemen's lavatory walking out through a wall where at one time there had been a door. The second, a middle-aged man, has been seen in the dining area near the fireplace. A preoccupation with trees here is shown in the village history. In 1586 John Brown was given permission to cut down an elm tree in the grounds of the Bell; in 1613 Robert Chandler was taken to court for carrying off an ash tree bough blown down in a storm and in 1642 John Young was arrested for felling an oak without a licence.

Jevington

(Map 6 page 9)

This Saxon village was built under a Neolithic causeway and called 'Geofinga tun'. Much smuggling took place here as James Pettit, or Jevington Jigg, worked from Birling Gap and Crowlink. Pettit, a local innkeeper, was deported to Botany Bay in 1799 for horse stealing. Nathanial Collier is recorded as dying here on 1 March 169 and a half. This was because of the confusion between the Roman Catholic calendar and the old style calendar of the English church.

EIGHT BELLS

Built in the 16th century, close to the South Downs Way, it opened as an inn over

200 years ago. Usually eight bells refers to the end of a naval watch and it was named by an ex-sailor landlord. There is a secret beer garden that is well known to hikers, and an inglenook fireplace and pre-decimal cash register. Local artists show their work here and some pieces can be bought. It was once a row of three cottages and has large exposed beams, dried hops and horse brasses,

John's Cross

(Map 7 page 10)

JOHN'S CROSS INN

One of the great pubs of Sussex, it opened in 1511, just before the Admiralty was founded in London. It is said to be haunted and on one occasion six mineral water bottles came out of a sealed packet and lined themselves up on the bar. Barrels in the cellar and furniture in the bar have moved about and ashtrays have suddenly tipped themselves up along the bar. The local villains were the Groombridge Gang with such names as 'Flushing Jack', 'Bulverhythe Tom', 'Tower', 'Old Joll', 'The Miller', 'Yorkshire George' and 'Nasty Face'. They terrorised the area but got their comeuppance in 1740 when they attacked the customs men at Robertsbridge. Local residents joined with the officers and beat the gang who were all rounded up and eventually hanged.

Kingston

(Map 2 page 7)

Alfred the Great required anyone breaking a solemn pledge to serve 40 days in prison at the 'Cyninges tun', meaning royal manor. This became 'Kyngeston' by 1312.

JUGGS

Many years ago, women carried fish from the markets in leather jugs called baskets and this 15th-century building is named after this. Brighton fishermen were also known as jugs. It is a tile-hung pub with small, ground floor windows and dormer windows. Inside it is as low beamed as one can get with leaning plaster walls stiffened with beams and many brass artifacts displayed, including a hunting horn. The inn sign shows a young fishwife filling the carrying baskets. In the 17th century a man's buttocks were known as 'double jugs'.

Kirdford

(Map 2 page 7)

This area belonged to a Saxon woman and was known as 'Cyneoryo'. It was recorded as 'Kinredeforde' in 1228.

HALF MOON

This pub was built in the mid-1600s to serve local people as a community building. It is on two storeys and has Sussex hung-tiles. There were additions and changes made by C.T. Woodridge in 1743, when he left his signature. Here there were workshops for wheelwrights, cartwrights, farriers, blacksmiths and a coffin maker from the old church opposite. The large inglenook fireplace was once used for smoking bacon and hams and still has a bake oven at one side. Restaurant tables nestle right into the inglenook. Nearby there is a village sign, dated 1937, which tells the tales of the village since the Bronze Age. Right opposite was a sign of admonishment reading 'Degradation of Drunkeness', but it is thought to apply to a bygone vicar rather than Half Moon customers.

Lambs Green

(Map 3 page 8)

LAMB INN

Often this pub name commemorates William Lamb, of the 16th century, who built conduits for the poor in London so they could have fresh water. Lamb was a choral musician who served as Gentleman of the Chapel to Henry VIII and was well known for his charitable works. Occasionally, when linked with the flag, the lamb has Christian connotations. This village pub is over 400 years old.

Lewes

(Map 6 page 9)

It was recorded as Laewe in AD 961 from the Saxon 'hlaew', meaning low hills, and had become 'Laewes' by 1065. After killing Thomas Becket at Canterbury, the four murderers fled to Old Malling Farm near Lewes. They put their murderous weapons on the table but the table rose up and threw the weapons to the ground, and at the Anne of Cleves Museum here there is

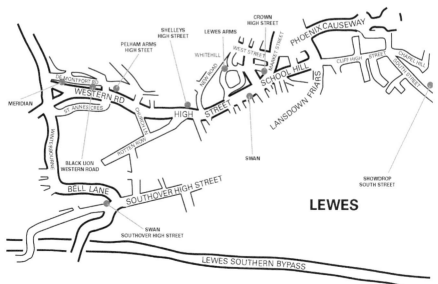

a slab of stone said to be the Malling Table. At nearby South Malling in 1636, John Harvard, founder of America's most famous university, was married to Ann Sadler, daughter of the rector of Ringmer. On the wall of the church is a copy of the entry from the church register.

BLACK HORSE, Western Road

The Black Horse is a former coaching inn with two bars and the name is 600 years old. It was also the nickname for the 7th Dragoon Guards in the 17th century because of the black collars and cuffs on their jackets and because they rode black horses. The public bar has a collection of photographs of the old town and a piano for singalongs. In 1810 it was described as having good stabling and was connected to racehorses.

CROWN INN, High Street

The Crown is the second most popular pub name after the Red Lion, and has been

so for 600 years. It showed loyalty to royalty that disappeared during the English civil war but returned afterwards during the reign of Charles II. In 1675 the Crown Inn opened its doors and the landlord then was Henry Townsend. It was known as the Black Lyon at this time but became the Crown in 1790, in the same year that the mutineers off the Bounty settled on Pitcairn Island, and the landlord then was Joseph Spittle. It is the headquarters of the Waterloo Society, one of the bonfire societies that plan the famous Lewes bonfire in November. William IV stayed here incognito when on holiday in Brighton.

LEWES ARMS,
Mount Place

This pub is a remarkable, curved-front building with three small but fascinating bars. In an upstairs room, the Lewes Folk Club meet. There are pictures on the walls by local artists. The pub is carved into the ramparts of the old Lewes Castle and there is a display of Beard's Brewery dray horse tack in the rear bar. In 1773 the landlord, John Spilsbury, made arrangements for his own funeral. He gave exact details of the coffin and named the six licensees he wanted to carry it. In 1954 one previous landlord, Mr W. Brown, was with Mr John Percy in Church Lane and both claim to have seen a flying saucer travelling faster than a jet plane that then disappeared in the direction of Crowborough.

MERIDIAN, Western Road
Built over 150 years ago as a canteen for the building workers on Lewes Prison, the Meridian is a long, white, one-storey building with black shuttering. The Greenwich Meridian line runs through it.

PELHAM ARMS, High Street
The pub was built in 1640, the year of the Short and Long Parliaments, but the oldest deeds for the pub only go back to 1758, which say 'Earlier documents missing'. A ghost in the cellar called George makes frequent appearances here. The inn sign carries the coat of arms of the Pelham family, one of whom fought at Agincourt. It has been known in the past as the Rose and the Dog and had extensive connections with horse racing. It is a long, mustard-coloured building with a large inglenook

fireplace and a settle dated 1706. Well known jockeys Fred Archer, George Fordham and Tom Cannon have stayed here.

SHELLEY'S HOTEL BAR, High Street

A Queen's Counsel, prosecuting at the quarter sessions, was lifted several inches from his bed during the night while staying here. It was the scene of a suicide many years ago and poltergeists are still believed to be active. It is named after the poet Percy Bysshe Shelley whose aunt once owned the place. Shelley was expelled from Oxford for writing a pamphlet on 'The Necessity of Atheism'. It is a 16th-century building with a Victorian bar. Shelley's started life as an inn called the Vine in 1562 and was involved in a Star Chamber dispute. John Pelland was the landlord in 1577 and this date is carved over the curved porch.

SNOWDROP, South Street

This pub was built on the site of a dreadful tragedy. In 1836 40 people lived in a row of houses underneath the cliffs here. One Christmas Eve, during the worst winter on record, snow had piled up on the cliffs and they had been told to leave because of a possible snowfall. Some refused and the snow crashed down on the cottages below. It buried the cottages and eight people died. The pub was named in memory of this incident. In the language of flowers, the snowdrop was made from a snowflake to comfort Adam and Eve after their expulsion from the Garden of Eden and indicates hope.

SWAN INN, Southover Road

The Swan Inn is a corner inn from the 18th century set in the historic area of Southover near Anne of Cleves' House. It is surrounded by houses with flint walls which indicate that the building is of a considerable age. It was once a barn and orchard owned by a yeoman and is now on three storeys with fine dormer windows. It was probably named the Swan after Anne of Cleves whose badge was a swan.

WHITE HART, High Street

The White Hart has been an important coaching inn since 1717, the year that John Law founded the Louisiana Company and the first Masonic Lodge opened in London. When Tom Paine (1737–1809) started his 'Age of Reason' he described his discussions here as 'the cradle of American Independence'. Paine, a former Revenue officer, lived in Lewes between 1768 and 1774 at a mediaeval inn called the Bull and was a member of the White Hart bowling club. While in North America, he advocated independence from Britain. The room where he held his discussions is now the Tudor or Sheriff's Room and is used by that official for the Lewes Crown Court. It has a copy of the American Constitution on the wall. William Cobbett stayed here during his travels. In the mid-1550s, some 17 men and women were burned at the stake in Lewes by judges who were trying to impose the authority of the Pope, and before execution the martyrs were kept in the mediaeval wine cellars of this inn. A previous landlord, William Verral, wrote the *Compleat System of Cookerie*. In 1807 Mad Jack Fuller ran a general election campaign from here and it cost him 2,000 dinners.

Lickfold

(Map 2 page 7)

The name of the village is from the Saxon 'leac falod', meaning garlic enclosure.

LICKFOLD INN

The Lickfold is an outstanding village inn that was the home of William de Lykfold in the 1330s. There is a ghost at the pub, a female, that has been seen on many occasions by landladies, and customers of a psychic bent have reported hearing and feeling her about the inn. There have been several tales of ghosts in the men's lavatory as well. Opened as an inn in the 1460s, it is of timber-frame construction with herringbone brickwork and in the large inglenook fireplace there are kitchen tools from years ago.

Lindfield

(Map 3 page 8)

One of the best kept villages in Sussex, Lindfield was named 'linda fel' in Saxon, meaning linden land where lime trees grow. In a charter of AD 765 it was called 'Lindefeldia'. There is a large pond here, popular with many fowl, that has its own Harbour Master.

WITCH

Opened in 1845, when the pneumatic tyre was invented by Robert Thomson, the witch still advertises 'good stabling'. It was not named after witches dancing at night or flying across the moon on broomsticks but after a brew known locally as 'Witches Brew', made by two sisters who once owned the pub. However, it is also possible that it was named after the wych elms that were cut down here for industry.

LINDEN TREE

For the delectation of all who love Sussex villages a journey here is a must. It is a small, main street pub surrounded by old-fashioned shops. Behind the Linden Tree there are the remains of a brewery. Linden is the old name for lime. It was once called the Old Stand Up because of its lack of seating. The landlord then, Edward Durrant, said he did not want people hanging around playing dominoes or lingering over a half-pint so he took away all furniture in 1906 and said: 'Let 'em stand up and drink up'.

Litlington

(Map 6 page 9)

The name derives from the Saxon 'Lyeteling tun', meaning the home of Liti – a diminutive man. In 1786 Mrs Maria Fitzherbert lived at Clapham House here and was secretly married, as Mr and Mrs Payne, to the Prince Regent who became George IV. In the 1880s, a white horse was cut into the downs above the village to attract tourists from Brighton. It is 90ft long and was covered up during World War Two.

PLOUGH AND HARROW

Dating from the 14th century, the pub was once a wattle and daub building but it has been extended and rebuilt over the years. It is a Grade II listed building and has a peg-tiled roof. There are carved settles and cut-down beer barrels to eat at. The Plough is an old pub name usually found in agricultural areas and sometimes written as the Plow. It is one of the most delightful pubs of the Sussex valleys and it is on the downs. There are grass-covered Saxon burial mounds here.

Lodsworth

(Map 2 page 7)

The Saxon village was called 'Lodeswuroa', meaning the enclosure of a man called Lod, and by 1272 was known as 'Lodesworth'. On one village cottage there is an old fire-mark that was issued by an insurance company who kept their own fire-fighting team before public fire brigades were set up.

HOLLIST ARMS

There has been a building here, probably an alehouse, since 1401, the year that Owen Glyndwr made his first bid for the independence of Wales. It takes its name from a local family and their crest is on the inn sign. It has a secluded garden and outside there is a spreading red chestnut tree with a seat all the way round it.

Lower Beeding

(Map 3 page 8)

Both Beedings were named after the 'Beadingas', meaning the people of Beada, and in AD 880 was known as 'aet Beadingum'.

THE CRAB TREE

Part of this inn is 400 years old and it was once used as a smuggler's den. It has an inglenook fireplace. Hilaire Belloc, a Sussex author, describes it in *The Four Men*, a book about his journey across the county with friends at the turn of the 19th century. In 1799 a party of soldiers appeared here asking for food, but there was nothing they fancied. However, one of the men saw a canary in a cage, asked how much, eventually paid half a guinea and then killed, cooked and ate the bird. (There is wider menu available today.)

Loxwood

(Map 2 page 7)

Loxwood was originally called 'locces wudu', meaning a patch of wood owned by a Saxon called Locc. In 1850 a group of Puritanical Evangelists arrived here, set up a store by the pond and founded the Society of Dependants, an austere group banning sport, theatre and music also known as the Cokelers because they were strictly teetotal. They raised 2,000 members and their chapel is still here in Spy Lane.

ONSLOW ARMS

This pub was built for navvies and workers on the canal joining London and

Chichester. It was also used as a horse changing station and was originally built by the Onslow family who lived nearby. The canal system was abandoned a century ago but work is now going ahead to restore part of it. It is an 18th-century inn with an inglenook fireplace and gardens right down to the canal. The old stables are still here and narrowboats are tied up behind the pub. Fishing permits are available at the bar.

Lurgashall

(Map 2 page 7)

The name derives from the Saxon 'Lutegares healh' from an early settler and it had become known as 'Lutegareshal' by 1224, shortly after the first poll tax was introduced in England.

NOAH'S ARK

This pub has stood here since 1450 and has never changed its name. The ark was a useful sign to have in the middle ages when *The Deluge* was shown as a religious mystery play. The ark was also used as the insignia of the Shipwrights' Company. It is situated in a beautiful village, found down narrow country lanes, with a fine village green where cricket is played and often concert and theatre groups perform. It is said that the inn took this name because there was once a pond outside that people

had to cross, giving the impression of animals going into the ark. Protector Cromwell trained his New Model Army on this green.

Malling

(*Map 6 page 9*)

BLACK LION

The Black Lion was an heraldic insignia referring to Queen Philippa of Hainault, wife of Edward III, and Owen Glendwr, the Welsh chief born in 1350. Originally this was the home of the village blacksmith, but it was converted to a pub over 170 years ago. It has a Tudor-style gable end.

Maplehurst

(*Map 3 page 8*)

WHITE HORSE

The White Horse is another bucolic delight with the longest single bar in Sussex. It was made from one piece of wood and measures 12ft 6in by 3ft. The landlord is a classic cars devotee and has some that can be hired for special occasions.

Mayfield

(*Map 5 page 9*)

Mayfield was recorded as 'maegoa', deriving from the name of the camomile-scented plant now called mayweed. The devil is said to have turned up in disguise here wanting a horse shoed but Saint Dunstan (then a village blacksmith while he spread the gospel) beat him to a pulp, and the Devil swore he would never enter a house again where there was a horseshoe above the door.

MIDDLE HOUSE

An oak-beamed inn dating from 1575, the Middle House has a frontage of nine Elizabethan windows and a prison room behind the bar. This was where one landlord kept his wife to 'correct her infidelities'. Four Protestants from Mayfield were condemned as heretics and taken to Lewes for burning. They are still remembered by Mayfield's Bonfire Boys and Belles, one of the oldest bonfire

societies in the country. The Mayfield gang, under Gabriel Tomkins, started by carrying out non-violent owling (wool smuggling by night) and had huge local support. The local farmers smuggled goods abroad and brought back brandy and silks. The Captain Swing Rioters, land workers demanding better pay, were put down by armed force in 1830 at Mayfield and many were imprisoned or transported to the colonies.

ROSE AND CROWN

This oak-beamed inn is almost 500 years old and is situated on the village green. The town sign shows the tongs that, according to the local story, pinched the devil's nose. As he took flight, he is said to have relieved the burns in the lakes of Tunbridge Wells. To this day the waters there taste of sulphur and have a reddish appearance. The Rose and Crown was a coaching inn and has pew-style seats, brick and painted walls, low ceilings and an inglenook fireplace.

Merston

(*Map 1 page 6*)

In 1274 the settlement was known as 'Mershtone', meaning a marshy farmstead.

KINGS HEAD

The inn sign shows both Henry VIII and Edward IV. The inn has stood here since 1562. It was a 17th-century coaching inn and the archway for coaches and horses still remains and the stables are now garages.

Midhurst

(Map 1 page 6)

From the Saxon 'hyrst', meaning a place amid wooded hills, Midhurst was recorded in 1186 as 'Middehurst'.

ANGEL

There is a superb Victorian walled garden at this former coaching inn. Dating back to the 16th century, it has a white-painted frontage. Nearby is Elizabethan House, which is a four-storey, timber-framed house. The inn was given its name by a group of Pilgrim Fathers on their way to Southampton, heading for America. During renovations a well was found dating from 1666.

SPREAD EAGLE

The American emblem is the white or bald-headed eagle, but the sign here goes back further than that. It was used by the Romans and was marched as a standard at the head of their legions. This inn takes the emblem from a local family who bear it on their coat of arms. Hilaire Belloc probably went over the top when he described it as

'that old and most revered of all prime inns of this world', but probably not by much. One part of the inn dates from about 1430, with half-timbering and lattice windows, and it was previously used as a hunting lodge. In the main bedroom there is a wig powdering room once used by travellers and a particularly fine Queen's Beam in the King's Room. Another part of the building dates from 1650 when a brick addition was made. Edward VII stayed at the hotel

on occasions and it has been patronised by royalty for the past 500 years.

SWAN INN

Over five centuries ago, in 1459, this inn was built on the square opposite the Spread Eagle, at the same time as the foundation of Glasgow University. A mural in the dining area is over 300 years old and was donated by the builders of St Anne's Hill when they stayed at the inn during the 16th century. At a nearby nunnery, in the 15th century, nuns were accused of gross immorality and spending holy money on feasting and hunting.

Netherfield

(Map 7 page 10)

Nether usually implies a lower or rear land but this comes from an ancient word 'nadder', which today has become adder. This was an area infested with snakes and was called 'naeddre feld'. A number of ancient words dropped the 'n' prefix as in apron and uncle although the phrase 'a present from nunc or nunkey' is still used.

NETHERFIELD ARMS

A long, white and ancient building with old wheels on the front, this pub has the most spectacular views over Sussex leading right down to the sea several miles away.

There is evidence to suggest that the well-clipped hedge in front is many centuries old.

Newhaven

(Map 6 page 9)

Fortified camps surrounded Newhaven from 250 BC and were occupied by the Saxon 'Mecingas'.

HOPE

In Victorian days, this was a row of terraces including two pubs, the Sea House and

the Hope, with two cottages in between. The first pub, the Sea House, and the cottages disappeared but the Hope remained and was rebuilt in the 1930s. It has a marvellous view over the harbour from the terrace and Newhaven Fort is high on the cliffs behind.

BRIDGE INN

The Bridge Inn is a long, cream building where French King Louis Philippe and his Queen stayed in 1848. It opened in 1620 as the New Inn, as the Pilgrim Fathers sailed to North America. The lounge is built to resemble a 20th-century liner and even has red and white lifebelts in it. The rear bar has an unusual ceiling of egg boxes and a mermaid is painted on one wall. One landlord, Thomas Tipper, brewed special ale for George IV when he was in Brighton.

Newick

(Map 5 page 9)

Newick was originally called 'Niwe wic', meaning new farm. It has a working village pump, erected by residents in 1897 to celebrate Victoria's jubilee.

BULL INN

It is no wonder that this pub contains a restless spirit, seen dressed as a priest or monk, as it was on the route for pilgrims as a resting place from Winchester to Canterbury. It was built in 1510, about the same time that the Gentlemen-at-Arms was established as Henry VIII's personal bodyguard. The inn sign is a painting of a real Hereford bull sold at auction for £17,000, a world record price then. It is also haunted by a blue, ball-shaped object that races across the room.

Ninfield

(Map 6 page 9)

This settlement was known as 'Niwnumenan felda', meaning newly taken land by early settlers. Wife sales were not uncommon in the 18th century and as a wife was legally her husband's property she could be sold on, providing it was done publicly and before witnesses. In November 1790 a man sold his wife to a journeymen for half a pint of gin, but the next day he changed his mind and bought her back for a whole bottle. Ninfield still has iron stocks and a whipping post, manufactured there in the early 1700s.

KING'S ARMS

The King's Arms is a charming roadside inn built in the Georgian style. The pub was once an alehouse for farmers and labourers who worked nearby, and it was originally opened by a local farmer. It was, at one time, on a dirt track through the village and is over three centuries old.

Normans Bay

(Map 6 page 9)

STAR INN

The building went up in 1402 when it was known as the Sluice House, just two years after Chaucer died. It houses an old grandfather clock that has not been moved since 1845. The men who lived here controlled the flow of the river that still flows through the pub garden, and there is a penny piece stuck in an upright beam showing the level reached by a flood in 1831. The pub is situated on the drained marshes of Pevensey Levels where the first reclamation started in 1282. It became the Star of Bethlehem in the 17th century, and by the 18th century it was controlled by smugglers and criminals. In 1828 some 200 smugglers started bringing their booty ashore and came face to face with the authorities, all heavily armed. A dreadful battle ensued and very few smugglers survived.

Northchapel

(Map 2 page 7)

This was once the centre of the glass and iron industries and had a charcoal factory. According to Charlotte Latham, in her book *Some West Sussex Superstitions*, a superstition originating from Northchapel was a cure for a person with weak eyes: they had to wear a live toad around the neck until the toad died.

HALF MOON INN

The Half Moon was built in 1576, at the same time that Drake was preparing for his round the world voyage in the Golden Hind. Famous cricketer Noah Mann was born in the village in 1756 and later became landlord of this pub. As a lark, he would pick up handkerchiefs from the ground while riding his horse at full gallop. He died when he fell into the pub fire and is buried in the churchyard, but his ghost still haunts the pub. One landlady, Mrs Wilkinson, was here for 61 years.

Northiam

(Map 7 page 10)

Northiam was once called 'heah hamm', meaning a northern hay meadow, and has the smallest house in Sussex, Smuggler's Cottage.

CROWN AND THISTLE

The pub name refers to the union between Scotland and England under James I in 1603. The thistle has been the emblem of Scotland since the eighth century. This is a 14th-century pub with resident ghosts. One female ghost is about 40, wears a long brown dress and bonnet-style hat and wanders around before disappearing through a wall. A more elegant apparition is that of a man wearing doublet and hose and a feather in his hat.

HAYES ARMS HOTEL

Queen Elizabeth I had food prepared here on her journey to Rye in 1573. The baking oven where this regal meal was prepared still exists in the large inglenook fireplace. In gratitude she left a pair of green damask shoes to the village. The resident indwells here include an elderly woman working her spinning wheel and a woman of 30 years old, dressed in grey with a white hat and holding something in her right hand. There have been reports of the spinning wheel actually moving itself across the room, and one guest reported a dreadful looking old woman bending over it and pulling it into the alcove.

Nutbourne, nr Pulborough

(Map 2 page 7)

This was known in Saxon as 'Hnutu burna', meaning a bourne or stream overhung with nut trees.

RISING SUN INN

Once a farmhouse over 500 years ago, the pub still retains an ivy-covered Georgian frontage. Entry is by way of railed steps. Found down a country lane, it is surrounded by old cottages, some thatched. The old stagecoach entrance displays early metal advertising boards. Inside there are wooden beams and floors and scrubbed tables. The rising sun was an heraldic device of Edward III, Richard III and many landed aristocrats. Once the village green was opposite the pub but this has now gone.

Nuthurst

(Map 3 page 8)

The name derives from the Saxon words 'hnutu hyrst', meaning nut tree wood.

BLACK HORSE

The Black Horse is a popular pub name from the 14th century and was once the insignia used by goldsmiths in Lombard Street. It was an old coaching inn on the Brighton to Horsham run and had previously been a row of 17th-century cottages. Hunting prints and old photographs adorn the walls and an inglenook fireplace warms the pub. There is a wealth of oak beams, flagstone floors and a wattle and daub wall. A small, stone bridge leads to a secluded garden.

Nyetimber

(Map 1 page 6)

Originally a Saxon village, it was recorded in the Domesday Book as 'Nitinbreham'.

LION HOTEL

The Lion Hotel was originally built in the 13th century and rebuilt in 1407. There used to be a tunnel a mile long connecting the inn with a former church, which was used by free traders and smugglers. There is a spy window on the top floor that was used to watch for the revenue men. An apparition is said to move through this inn between three and six in the morning. A rustling of heavy gowns has been heard and witnesses have seen a tall woman in a grey or blue dress. She is said to have a particularly radiant smile. She is supposed to have been murdered here because she knew too much about some criminal activities.

Offham (Arundel)

(Map 2 page 7)

The name originates from the Saxon for a watermeadow in the bend of a river, 'Offan hamm'.

BLACK RABBIT

This is the only pub in England with this name. It can be found down a narrow lane opposite the river. It is 200 years old and was used by navvies and bargees working the local canals. It was also once involved in smuggling. The first landlord was John Olliver in 1804 and it stayed in this family for 70 years. There used to be croquet lawns and an archery pitch and it was a fashionable meeting place for Edwardians. The old boathouses are now the restaurant. At nearby Arundel Castle, there are four ghosts: a white bird, a Stuart period dandy and a boy and girl.

Offham (Lewes)

(Map 6 page 9)

Again from the Saxon for a watermeadow, it is situated on the Ouse and was called 'woh hamm', becoming Wocham in 1092, but it became Offham by common pronunciation.

CHALKPIT

The pub is three centuries old and was built into an old chalkpit. There are several similarly named pubs throughout the country, named in memory of the men who worked in the chalkpits. There are still the remains of the old lime kilns nearby. There is also a double railway tunnel, built in 1809, running under the main road, which led to a 400ft drop to a wharf on the River Ouse.

Pett

(Map 7 page 10)

It was known as 'Pette' in 1195. Just off Pett shoreline is a submarine forest of trees including oak, beech and pine. The stumps can be seen when the tide is out.

ROYAL OAK

Pett was without this pub for 70 years when it was closed by the landowner because she disapproved of the intemperate ways of the villagers. She turned it into a temperance hotel but it later reopened as the Royal Oak. In 1974 the wreck of the Anne was found in sands on Pett Shore. She had run aground and was burned out by the captain after the sea battle with the Dutch off Beachy Head. There is also the Royal Military Canal nearby. In 1804, when threatened by a French invasion the 30ft-wide canal was built by the government to keep them at bay, and it was the greatest defence folly of that century. The pub has one open bar, oak-beamed with a large inglenook fireplace.

TWO SAWYERS

The Two Sawyers is a 15th-century building that was once an old ale house, butcher's

shop and forge. It has low beams, large inglenook fireplaces at each end of the restaurant and a boules pitch. The sawyers were unskilled workmen who were not allowed to be in the guilds of carpenters, joiners and shipwrights. There are two small bars with fine oak support beams, a large collection of old saws and a fascinating alcove. The inn is embowered in ivy and flowers in the summertime.

Petworth

(Map 2 page 7)

In AD 785 'Eadwulf', last king of the South Saxons, granted land here to St Peter's Church, Selsey. Then it was known as 'Peartingwyrth' and originally as 'Peota woro', meaning farm of Peota. A Petworth woman, Hannah Ward, born in 1787, followed the British army as a camp follower and was present at Waterloo and Quatre Bras. She was the wife of a private in the 35th Regiment of Foot and was buried at Hunston churchyard.

ANGEL

The Angel is a five centuries old town inn and at one time there was a hole in the ceiling to allow smoke out from the inglenook fire that is still extant. An elderly woman who was waiting for a friend here saw her crash down the stairs to her doom and was so shocked that she died herself within a couple of days. Every now and again, she is seen sitting at the inglenook fireplace in old-fashioned garb.

Pevensey

(Map 6 page 9)

In AD 947 it was known as 'Pefenesea', from the Saxon word meaning Pefen's river, and in the Domesday Book was called 'Pevenesel'. In the third century the Romans built on an earlier stronghold to protect against Saxon invasions, and the sea has now retreated and left the ruined castle inland. It became part of the Cinque Ports as a Limb of Hastings and had its own mint from 1342. Elizabeth I ordered the castle to be demolished but fortunately this did not occur.

ROYAL OAK

Standing opposite the castle gates, this large pub was used as an emergency centre for firefighters. It opened in 1853, as Livingstone discovered the Victoria Falls. Nearby is the Court House in the Liberty of Pevensey, dating back to Saxon times, and a marvellous little museum with cells on the ground floor and stories of smugglers and other history on the walls. The last woman to be locked up in the cells was Betty Breach, for assaulting her husband in the New Inn (now the Smuggler's) and being abusive towards the landlord. Another woman caught stealing calico here was whipped through the streets 'until her back be bloodied'.

SMUGGLER'S INN

This is one of the most important historic sites in England for it was here that William the Conqueror landed, with 700 boats, in 1066. Andrew Borde, a monk, scholar and physician to Henry VIII, lived in the town, and is best known for his work *Merry Tales of the Mad Men of Gotham*. The pub is haunted by a somewhat benevolent spirit. The landlady said often when they think they have locked up for the night there is a bang on the door and when they check again the door is not bolted. A former landlady made rope for local fishermen. Inside the entrance is a prie-dieu (a praying desk) with no indication that it is for penitent imbibers.

Piltdown

(Map 5 page 9)

PILTDOWN MAN

This is a roadside inn named after the 'Eoanthrapos Dawsoni', the Piltdown Man. In 1912 Charles Dawson, a Lewes solicitor, was on Piltdown Common watching a gravel-digging gang when he claimed to have found part of a skull. He unearthed the upper part of the skull and half a lower jaw and showed it to archaeologists and scholars who maintained that this was the so-called 'missing link' in evolution, but in the 1950s this was proved to

be a hoax. The inn sign shows something half man and half ape. It was originally the Lamb Inn.

Playden

(Map 7 page 10)

This village was built on a play pasture where young farm animals frisked. In Saxon It was known as 'Plega denn' and by 1086 had become 'Pleindena'.

PEACE AND PLENTY

The Peace and Plenty is a truly delightful name for a pub and this one looks as though it really stands up to its name. Peace and Plenty became a fairly common name for pubs after the wars in France in the early 1800s. Shakespeare also refers to this in one of his plays about 'peace and plenty throughout the land'.

Plumpton

(Map 4 page 8)

The name comes from 'Plumme tan', meaning a Saxon farmstead where plum trees grow. On nearby Buckland Bank there is a famous Bronze Age settlement. Once there was a witch in the village, Old Martha, said to be 100 years old and very rich. An early writer on Sussex maintains that she chased him down Barracks Hill running backwards and screaming loudly with a knife in each hand.

HALF MOON

Opened in 1842, as the Opium Wars ended in China and Hong Kong was leased to Britain, this was a staging inn for coaches and mail horses on the Ditchling to Offham turnpike. In the bar, there is a brick-built log fire and a 3ft by 1.5ft painting, by Dick Leech, of 130 regulars from 1978. Outside is a patio with rustic tables, embowered in wisteria and clematis.

Polegate

(Map 6 page 9)

Once a rural backwater, it was referred to, at the time of Elizabeth I, as

'Powlegate Corner' or 'Poolgate'. Cyclists going from Polegate to Heathfield through Hailsham can find an excellent cycle track on the Cuckoo Trail, developed from the old Polegate-Heathfield railway line that was abandoned in 1964.

DINKUM

Originally called the Polgate Inn, it took its present name during World War One when there was a colonial service camp nearby. The Australian contingent described it as 'fair dinkum' and the name stuck. Once it had an inn sign showing an Australian solider in a large bush hat, by Julian Bell, but this has been replaced by a signboard showing a World War One nurse helping a soldier. The Lewes-Polegate tollgate opened near here in 1819. The former railway station is now a pub, the Old Polegate Station Inn.

HORSE AND GROOM

Built in 1835, at the appearance of Halley's Comet and when the electric telegraph was invented, it has had a chequered career, moving in 1930 and then again in 1948. It was an original alehouse and in the 1841 census the innkeeper was noted as Henry Tutt. It is a curious mixture of a Victorian building of Sussex brick with mock-Tudor facings, small paned windows and one door with an enormous stone lintel. On two panels there are paintings of a horse and groom copied from work by J.F. Herring. Outside is a spreading oak tree with tables and chairs underneath it, and there is a super view of the South Downs. Not far away there is a red, metal shed, which is all that is left of an airship station built during World War One. At Donkey Bottom there are mooring posts for the airships used to patrol the coastline.

Portslade

(Map 4 page 8)

Portslade was recorded as 'Porteslage' in 1086 and had become 'Porteslade' by 1179.

STAG'S HEAD

The pub dates from 1674, the same year that John Milton died. It has a flint façade and contains a bust of the ghost that haunts it. A man who spotted him described him to an art student who then built the bust that now rests on the bar. The ghost has been seen on many occasions and usually appears in the cellar. He has a quirky sense of humour and changes over the beer lines from full barrels to empty ones.

Poynings

(Map 4 page 8)

Poynings was recorded in Saxon in AD 960 as 'Puningas', meaning a warrior, 'Puna'.

ROYAL OAK

The Royal Oak is covered with vine and wisteria in the summertime. It has a wood-burning stove at each end of the bar and an exotic ghost is in residence. A former landlord, a flamboyant fellow who used to wear tartan tunics, can be recognised by his clothing as he appears from time to time walking through the bar and into the kitchen. A barman said that the apparition actually looked at him and gave a civil nod as he went past. One couple reported being awakened at three o'clock in the morning to hear sounds of a merry party going on in the bar, with conversation and glasses clinking, but when they went down the bar was empty.

Pulborough

(Map 2 page 7)

In Saxon the village was known as 'Pole Beorg', which meant the mound near the pools.

ODDFELLOWS ARMS

The Oddfellows Arms is a four centuries old, roadside inn below the level of the present road, and it was once a coaching inn. It is tile-hung with rough plastering and ancient beams inside. The name refers to the Independent Order of Oddfellows, a social and benevolent society, whose name is said to derive from a remark made by a founding member. Some years ago, a landlord took over here and found, hidden away upstairs, a cockpit left as last used. There were still pegs for tethering the birds and it was soiled by their droppings and feathers.

Punnett's Town

(Map 5 page 9)

Punnett's Town was named after Anthony Pannet of Herstmonceux in 1645. Author Rudyard Kipling wrote about the windmill here in many of his stories. It was called Cherry Clack and he named it Cherry Black Windmill.

THREE CUPS INN

The Three Cups is a delightful 17th-century hostelry that has the date 1696 written on a beam over the fireplace. This was the year of the first settlement in New Jersey. There is a low-beamed bar where snuff is available and several ghosts are in residence at this curiously named inn. On the inn sign there are three stirrup cups but the name refers to a time when the building was part of the watershed dividing three streams. 'Cups' is an old Sussex word for source of stream. There is a stone bust of a previous landlord made by a customer who could not afford to pay his bill here. The present landlord's car has the registration plate 'C3UPS' as a tribute to his pub.

Pyecombe

(Map 4 page 8)

The name comes from the Saxon 'Peac cumb', meaning the peak valley. A local smithy made shepherds' crooks here, which were exported worldwide and used for ceremonial occasions by the bishops of Great Britain.

PLOUGH INN

Because of the number of fatal accidents on the main road here, a morgue was set up in the Plough cellar in the early 1930s. There have been reports of several apparitions being seen over the years, one being a nun in a grey habit with whom several customers have come to face to face in the ladies' lavatory. Glasses and bottles have come off shelves and, even on windless nights in the summertime, curtains have suddenly been ripped down with such force that the rails and fixings have come down too. One customer said they saw a woman in a black dress and white pinafore standing behind the landlady, who then suddenly disappeared.

Ringmer

(Map 6 page 9)

Once called 'hring mere', meaning the ring mere or circular marsh pool, it had become known as Ringmere by 1276. At South Malling, William Penn married Guliemea Springett, the daughter of a Ringmer man, and John

Harvard married Ann Sadler, the daughter of the rector of Ringmer, and the village sign incorporates both William Penn and John Harvard.

COCK INN

The cock is an old pub name from the 14th century and was later used to indicate that cockfighting took place there. Sometimes it also meant that they served cock-ale, a mixture of ale and the jelly of a boiled cock bird. It was built in 1450, at the same time of Cade's rebellion. On the exterior, the pub has white weatherboarding and inside there are open fires and naval prints adorning the walls. Daniel Defoe stayed here occasionally and wagons stopped here to get a 'cock horse' or additional horse power to get them up a long hill on the Brighton to Tunbridge coach run. There is a picture of Timothy Tortoise by Gilbert White, a naturalist, on the signpost to the parish church near here. Timothy came from Virginia, US, in 1734 and was sold at Chichester Harbour for half a crown.

Robertsbridge

(Map 7 page 10)

Robert de St Martin, a Norman nobleman, founded a Cistercian monastery here with a bridge over the Rother, and the village name was recorded as 'Pons Roberti' in 1199.

GEORGE INN

The George is a noble inn facing a small village green and ancient cottages. Licensees in the past have reported hearing curious bumps and bangs and footsteps coming from empty rooms. These strange sounds always occur after there has been a wedding reception as the ghost, affectionately known as Georgina, does not seem to like weddings. Once when a member of the staff was in the kitchen she saw the door slowly open but no-one was there and although it was a very hot day the temperature dropped so much that she started shivering.

SEVEN STARS

A pub has stood here for about 500 years near to the Cistercian monastery. The seven stars was a well known sign in the middle ages and referred to the celestial crown of the Virgin Mary. Over the years, there have been sightings of a ghostly, red monk in his earthly perambulations. It is believed that the original building may date back to the time of Richard I. Horace Walpole stayed here in the mid-1750s and was surprised to find it was the haunt of smugglers, highwaymen, prostitutes and other 'ne'er do wells'. In the nearby church of St Mary the Virgin is the grave of Peter Sparkes who died in 1683 and was said to be 127 years old.

Rodmell

(Map 6 page 9)

Below the South Downs, Rodmell was originally called 'reada mydle' in Saxon, named after the local red soil. At the time of James I, mulberry trees were grown here and the area was famous for its silk industry. At one time most houses were owned by the Marquess of Abergavenny and had an 'A' written on them.

ABERGAVENNY ARMS

A delightful old coaching inn dating from 1650, when coffee came to England, named after the Abergavenny family. It is a corner inn on the main road with a large garden. Nearby is Monks House: a 17th-century, weatherboarded house where Virginia Woolf and her husband, Leonard, lived from 1919 until she took her own life in 1941 by drowning in the River Ouse.

Rotherfield

(Map 5 page 9)

In AD 880 it was described as 'aet Hyroerafelda', meaning at the field of the cattle. A woman who fought for the rights of women to practise medicine spent part of her life here. Sophia Louisa Jex-Blake studied medicine and surgery in the United States but had to challenge the law in the courts to qualify in England. She was the first woman doctor in this country, in 1877, and died in Rotherfield aged 72.

KING'S ARMS

Every Midsummer Eve a girl who used to live at the pub makes an appearance here. Stories abound of footsteps running up and down the stairs and icy blasts. Even more curious, just bare feet have been spotted dancing in a corridor. A miserable old miller hanged himself here and also haunts the pub. Samuel Pepys stayed here and claims to have seen some odd things happening. The building is ancient and was, at one time, a tythe barn.

Rottingdean

(Map 4 page 8)

The Saxon name for the village was 'Rotinga dene', meaning the valley of Rota's people. Author Rudyard Kipling lived at The Elms for five years, and the beautiful Kipling Gardens are here. From the mid-1700s, it was a hive of smuggling activity under the Rottingdean Gang who used the tunnels between the houses and pubs. Vicar Dr Thomas Hooker was their lookout. Rudyard Kipling wrote 'Four and twenty ponies trotting through the dark' about these men. Before the days of electricity and telegrams, a German bank clerk moved here. His name was J. Reuter and he set up a pigeon post service to bring in financial news from abroad. This later became Reuters, the worldwide news agency. The village was the first place in Sussex to use an electric light.

BLACK HORSE

The Black Horse opened in 1515, about the same time Henry VIII chartered Trinity House, and was once known as the Black Hole. It is timber-framed with plastered walls and the lounge was once a blacksmith's forge. Between two bars, there is a fascinating snug bar.

Rowhook

(Map 2 page 7)

Rowhook is a 14th-century village whose name has not changed and means rough hook or spur of hill.

CHEQUERS

Built as a pub 600 years ago, it was called the Chequer after a tree that produced red berries in the autumn, which were dried and eaten. The old flagstones still remain in

the bar. There are low beams, old settles and wooden tables, open fires and paintings of local people inside. It has a long, black carved bar. The entrance is covered in honeysuckle, and outside there is a coach lamp and a pillory used for the 'wicked ones'. It is situated at the road junction of the old Roman road called Slave Street.

Rushlake Green

(Map 6 page 9)

A watercourse with rushes ran through the village and because of this it was recorded as 'Rysshelake' in 1537 and by 1567 had become 'Ruslake Grene'.

HORSE AND GROOM

Once a 16th-century farmhouse, the Horse and Groom opened as a pub in 1650, during the English Civil War. It overlooks the village green and has low beams and an open fire. A gun collection is displayed in the Gun Room restaurant. In 1803 the following statement was recorded relating to this pub: 'Buried John Pinyon, aged 44. Death by wrestling with a person by the name of Dan at the Horse and Groom, who, by a trip or kick, broke his leg, which brought on a fever which seized his brain.' Many years ago two human skulls were taken to this pub and later when a landlord tried to dispose of them they started screaming and turned the beer sour. No-one knows what eventually happened to these bony indwells.

Rusper

(Map 3 page 8)

This was an old forest area named by the Saxons as 'Ruh spaer', meaning the rough enclosure.

STAR INN

Just into Sussex, this pub is over 500 years old and was once a coaching inn. Now and again a shadowy man is seen sitting at a stool with a pint pot in his hand and when he does there is trouble with the beer lines and lights go on and off. It is an imposing

corner pub named after a religious symbol, which refers to the star of Bethlehem or the Virgin Mary.

PLOUGH INN

Situated in the centre of the village, the Plough is five centuries old and was once owned by the Nuns of Rusper who gave food and shelter to passing pilgrims. There is a very old chimney at the pub, built from Horsham stone tiles, and it is a traditional, one-bar pub with beams. In 1793 local villagers are said to have killed a pig here weighing 116 stone, the weight of 10 average men. In 1840 workmen came across the bodies of five sisters of an earlier priory here and they were reburied near the present church. In the church there is a tablet dedicated to Lucy Broadwood, a famous folksong collector.

Rustington

(Map 2 page 7)

The name Rustington came from 'Rustas tun', which meant Rusta's farmstead. The term 'rusta' was also applied to red-haired folk.

FLETCHER ARMS

Named after John Fletcher the dramatist, it is a large corner pub with local photographs and bric-a-brac on display. A young man was hanged in the pub many years ago and his ghost is said to haunt this place. It is a large Victorian building next door to a railway station. The old barn was once part of the post office and was used for stagecoach repairs.

Rye

(Map 7 page 10)

Rye is one of the most exquisite towns of Sussex with cobbled streets, ancient monuments and many pubs over a small area. Built on a promontory overlooking the sea, it was known originally as 'aet paere iege', meaning at the island, and Ria and Rya in the mid-12th century. In the 15th and 16th centuries, Rye's prosperity as one of the Cinque Ports disappeared as the sea receded. In 1742 John Breads was hanged here for murdering Allan Grebell whom he mistook for the Mayor of Rye, James Lamb. As he stabbed Grebell, Breads shouted: 'Butchers should kill Lambs'. He was landlord of the Flushing Inn here at the time. In the town centre there is an 18th century water pumping house that has been converted into a public lavatory.

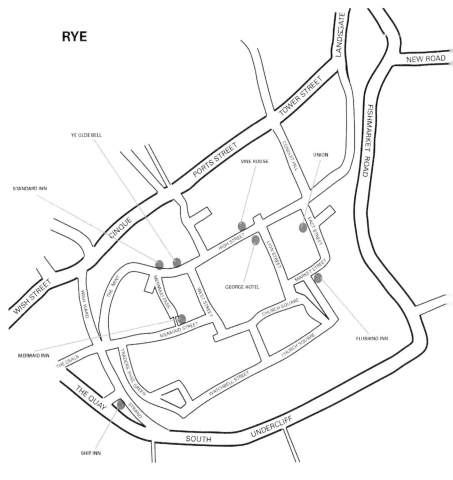

FLUSHING INN, Market Street

The Flushing Inn dates from 1200 but the original building was destroyed in a fire after the French attack in 1377. Only the Norman barrel-vaulted cellar still remains.

In the 1850s, the Flushing Inn was divided into three parts. In 1901 a wall painting from the time of Edward VI (1547–54) was found here and is now displayed in the restaurant, after being restored by Tom Organ in 1997. There are two theories as to where the name originates from. One is that it is named after after the Dutch port of Vlissingen. The other is that as the street it is on was once called The Butchery and the old English name for butchers was 'fleshers' the pub became known as the Fleshers Inn, which was corrupted to Flushing over time.

GEORGE HOTEL, High Street

The George hotel first opened during the Tudor period but it was rebuilt during Georgian times. It was on a coaching run and the George was the terminus for one famous coach, *Diligence*. In the past, parliamentary election results were announced from the balcony and the newly elected Mayor would throw a shovelful of hot coins to the public from the pub, but this ceased before World War Two. Rye was famous for the Bonfire Boys who would march through the streets, followed by terrible rioting. During one of these riots a police officer was thrown on to a bonfire and died from his injuries.

MERMAID INN,

Mermaid Street

Built in 1156 and rebuilt in 1426, this black and white timbered inn is one of the oldest in the country. Old ship's timbers were used in the construction and there are also some chairs carved from them, one in the shape of a goat. A large step-in fireplace runs along one wall. Two ghosts have been seen here, fighting a duel with swords. Dressed in 16th-century clothing, one has been seen to stab the other and drag his corpse across the room. Another local ghost is that of a monk, Cantator, who eloped with a local girl, Amanda, in

1385. They were caught and walled up to die. His magnificent voice was turned into a turkey gobble as a further punishment and he is still with us in Turkey Cock Lane. Smugglers and 'ne'er do wells' used this pub, particularly the Hawkhurst Gang, and Elizabeth I once stayed here. During restoration work, many hiding places for contraband, a concealed well and a stairway to a secret passage were found.

SHIP INN, Strand Quay

Down among the old warehouses on the river estuary, the Ship Inn has been in business for 500 years. As part of the ancient Cinque Port of Rye, the inn was used to store confiscated contraband as the Lord Warden's depot. On an outside wall is a list of revenue cutters and coast blockade boats used to pursue the smugglers in the 18th century. It is a large inn, surrounded by antique and bric-a-brac shops, with a beamed bar and much panelling.

STANDARD INN, The Mint
Built in 1420, the Standard Inn is a large, single bar with many old houses and shops around it. It is timber-framed with the walls stripped from them becoming partitions and room dividers. There are low ceilings, a bricked floor, an open fire and a low, L-shaped bar. Sometimes a Standard pub is named after the Battle of the Standard at Northallerton in 1138, but this was named because the battle standard included the flags of three saints on it. This is a must-see pub as there are very few like it left. It is a well known folk music centre.

UNION INN, East Street
The Union is a reference to a political union or important marriage. Built on a hill and almost next door to Rye Museum, it is haunted by the unhappy soul of an unmarried mother who worked here and fell downstairs, breaking her neck, many years ago. The other haunting is by a soldier in old-fashioned uniform, seen sitting in a bar. In a glass-fronted space in a wall, some bones of a child were found and some believe they may be connected with the unmarried mother.

WHITE VINE HOUSE, High Street
The White Vine House is a timber-framed inn built over mediaeval, vaulted cellars in the town centre. When it was a private residence, it was occupied by local historian William Holloway and the Mayor of Rye, Charles Pix Meryon, in the 19th century. An even earlier version of the building was called the Whyte Vyne Inn. A wicked little poltergeist lives here and spends much time upsetting the kitchen. Carrots are mixed into the onion bag and sugar put in with the potatoes.

WILLIAM THE CONQUEROR, Rye Harbour

The pub was named after William the Conqueror, who landed some way down the coast from here. He had been promised the English throne but in January 1066 the Saxon prince, Harold, was crowned instead, and the famous battle took place in

October at Senlac, north of Hastings, where Harold was killed. William ordered 'the Grand Inquisition of Lands Act of 1086' to be commissioned (the Domesday Book), which has been of vast, historical importance ever since. Considering his importance in English history, there are surprisingly few pubs named this, even in this area. Once a fisherman's cottage, the inn sign is of a silver penny from that time. The long bar is known as the Mess Room and it contains a forged iron screen showing a Norman on horseback wielding a war-axe. Outside there is a World War Two mine used to collect money for distressed mariners.

YE OLD BELL, The Mint This pub has stood here since 1430, at the time when Joan of Arc was battling against the English, and Elizabeth I once stayed here. Smugglers used a revolving door system here, to deliver their goods into a cupboard, so no-one would know who they were. This system was also used in the Spanish convents, to deliver food and goods, so they had no contact with anyone from the outside. One beam in the pub is said to be made from a tree that was growing in the exact spot where the pub now stands.

Scaynes Hill

(Map 3 page 8)

The village is named after a former owner, and was originally called 'Skerns Hill' in 1586.

FARMERS

The Farmers has a most impressive sweeping entrance and inside there are dark oak beams and an open fire with a large set of bellows. Pillsticks, used to keep open the mouths of large animals as they are given medicine, and a set of clogs, worn by carthorses to protect their feet on the roads, are kept on display here. The nearby town of

Haywards Heath was named after a highwayman called Hayward who used this village pub.

Seaford

(Map 6 page 9)

Romans settled in Seaford and used it for sea communications to the Continent. Alfred the Great had a palace at West Dean and used the area to house naval fleets that fought against the Vikings. The Black Death came to Seaford in 1348, and by 1357 there were not enough people to defend the town against French ravages. Since 1562 the people of Seaford have been known as 'cormorants' or 'shags' because of their abilities for looting and setting up lights to lure ships aground. There was once a ford here to cross the river, near the sea, but a storm in 1579 altered the course of the river and because of this it became less prosperous and had decayed by 1592. In 1795 starving soldiers in nearby barracks looted a sloop, *Lucy*, of 300 sacks of grain intended for export. After a court-martial, two were executed and four given 150 lashes. One executed soldier, Edward Cooke, still haunts Newhaven Fort.

OLD PLOUGH

The pub was opened in the 1850s as a coaching inn for passengers arriving from Lewes. It is next door to the parish church, which is a curious mixture of Norman and more recent architecture. When owned by George Lower, born in Seaford in 1821, it was called the Old Plough and Stables. In 1870 he became a coal merchant and ran his business from the Plough, becoming the Old Plough in 1877. There are a number of bars and a large terrace for al fresco eating.

WELLINGTON

The Wellington is a 17th-century former coaching inn standing on what used to be the old quayside of the Cinque Port. It was originally called the New Inn and changed its name when there was a newspaper report of a mysterious visitor (Wellington) to the inn in 1845. The Iron Duke often visited the town to review his troops and plan their embarkation for France and Spain.

Sedlescombe

(Map 7 page 10)

Around the green here are 16th and 17th century half-timbered cottages, and the name is from the Saxon term for a settlement in a valley, 'Setles cumb'. The Battle of Hastings took place only a few miles away. There was a gunpowder mill here, and in December 1764 four men died in an explosion there. The road through the village follows the route of the original Roman road.

QUEEN'S HEAD

The Queen's Head is an old pub on the green of this ancient settlement. For many years local residents suffered from the predations of Norman invaders. Once the

property of the Abbot of Battle, it was first licensed as an inn in 1523. As a coaching inn, it was also the turning point on the Eastbourne route. Over a century ago a pot of 3,000 coins from the reign of Edward the Confessor was found nearby and is thought to have been hidden by King Harold before the battle of Hastings. Interestingly, it appears that Harold was not shot through the eye at all, as legend has it. It is now believed that this story was invented some 15 years later as he had, in fact, been hacked to death. The arrow story was symbolic as it was then the punishment for perjury and treason.

Shoreham

(Map 4 page 8)

In Saxon this was 'scora ham', meaning a bank or shore homestead. It become 'Sorham' in 1073 and 'Nooua Sorham' in 1235. In 1457 a document refers to the port as 'Hulkesmouth alias Shorham', perhaps referring to a wreck in the harbour. I am indebted to Mrs Emma Goldstein, now of Barcombe, for some of these pub stories.

CROWN AND ANCHOR

Once a wooden figurehead of St George decorated the front of the nearby Royal George, and it was given to Eric Wardroper of the Crown and Anchor when it closed. This crashed down in the 1920s and was replaced by a statue of a bold pirate standing on the prow of a boat. There are a number of tales connected to this pub, one of which is a story of a French girl, brought ashore by a sailor and then abandoned, who worked here as a serving wench and then committed suicide by throwing herself from a rear window. She still haunts the pub. Another tells of three unwelcome customers who appeared at the pub and were barred. They returned the next day with three huge bags of confetti that they threw everywhere and it could not be cleared for weeks. Landlord Eric Wardroper was famous for his beef sandwiches and always kept a rib of beef at the end of the bar. When the rib was finished he threw it into the River Adur. One morning a man on the nearby footbridge thought he saw a body in the river and called the police. Eric received a severe rebuke from the health authorities.

MARLIPINS

Marlipins was built in 1725 next to a 12th-century building, Marlipins Museum, in Moddle Street (formerly Moderlove Street). It is named after a board game, dating from the 14th century, called merels. This was a game between two players,

using pegs. Originally Old French, the name gave rise to the words miracle, moral, and morris.

RED LION INN

The Red Lion is an old coaching inn from the 16th century where phantoms have been seen, not surprisingly as part of the building was once a monastery. It is a typical period pub with low beams and there is an old inglenook fireplace and roofing tiles made from Horsham stone. Tales abound of a murderer who was hanged for grisly crimes and still haunts part of Shoreham. He is said to visit certain homes and tries to strangle people as they lie in their beds. The pub is mentioned in Tennyson's *Rizpah* as the place where a convicted murderer was taken away and hanged.

ROYAL SOVEREIGN

This is the oldest pub in Shoreham, situated in what was Modderlove Street in mediaeval times, and it has a green-tiled frontage. The cellar is carved out of chalk and there are pockets hollowed out for wines and spirits. Below the cellar is a shaft leading down to the river, which may have been a mediaeval rubbish chute. Once Tom Sayers, the Sussex bare-knuckle fighter, trained in the room above the bar. Captain Henry Roberts, who sailed with Captain Cook in the South Seas, lived nearby.

SCHOONER

Smugglers used a secret tunnel down to the nearby waterfront and beach from this pub. Many years ago, a little girl and her nanny were drowned in the cellars when they were cut off by a rising tide. A former licensee woke up to find her hair being stroked, and a woman has been seen walking in the cellars with a child. Two mediums were called in to investigate the phenomenon and one of them fell down in a swoon and started speaking like a child. A bar manager saw a strange white light about 3ft across. He described the outer edge as electric blue and then saw a small red-haired child, about six years old, on the floor with her hands on her face.

Shortbridge

(Map 5 page 9)

Known as 'Shirtebreg' in 1297, Shortbridge was a bridge over a tributary to the River Ouse.

PEACOCK INN

The Peacock is set back from the roadside and there are two 200-year-old yew trees here, clipped to perfection. Built in the 1600s and hardly changed on the exterior, it overlooks a pleasant garden. Inside it is low-beamed with part wood-panelled walls and a carved, wooden bar. Furnishings are rural and simple. This pub name offers great opportunities to sign writers, and the peacock was occasionally used for heraldic significance, as in the arms of the Dukes of Rutland.

Sidlesham

(Map 2 page 7)

Sidlesham was named after a Saxon warrior and farmer, 'Sidelse ham', as it was his home in AD 630.

ANCHOR INN

The Anchor is a large eight centuries old inn, situated at a crossroads. It was once leased to Diones Geerle for a rental of eight pence for 1,000 years. Nearby, there are 18th-century thatched houses, a 13th-century church and the wild bird hospital. This hospital was started by Dennis Fenter when he hand-reared an injured sparrow in 1971, and Patrick Moore is now a vice-president.

CRAB AND LOBSTER

This 15th-century inn is close to the quay and is said to be haunted. It has two bars leading off from a stone-flagged hallway and both have open log fires. One bar counter is in the shape of a boat and is decorated with brass portholes and rope. It has a pleasant 1950s feeling to it. Pagham Harbour emerged here in 1345 when a large area of land was swamped by the sea. Out on the western side of the harbour there is a haven for birds and over 180 different species have been recorded there.

Sidley

The name comes from the Saxon 'sid leah', meaning the wide clearing.

NEW INN

High above a village green, the New Inn is a long, white-painted building on two storeys, dating from 1365. There has been some extra-ordinary activity experienced at this pub, believed to be poltergeists. Items go adrift, footsteps are heard and a mist sweeps along the upper floor. A child woke up one night and followed a light that led her to a woman who disappeared before her very eyes.

Slindon

(Map 2 page 7)

In Saxon Slindon was called 'slinu dun', meaning the hill by the slope, and in 1086 it was known as 'Eslindone'.

NEWBURGH ARMS

Built on National Trust property, this is one of the few privately owned buildings in the village. Opened in the 1750s, it was named after a local family who owned Slindon Estate. It is a village centre pub and has a large bar with beams and a log fireplace. One generous landlord, Frank Fleet, entertained carters with hot gin so well that they could not harness their horses. In the local church there is an effigy of Sir Anthony St Leger of 1539, the only wooden one in Sussex.

SPUR

The Spur is a former coaching inn that was once called Sir George Thomas. It is over 400 years old and has huge open fire places. It is not a common name for a pub and it is named after the pricking tool used in horse riding to encourage the horses to go faster. They come in five types: box, dropped hammerhead, polo, racing and rowelled. Famous cricketer Richard Newland was born in Slindon and is said to be the father of modern cricket.

South Harting

(Map 1 page 6)

Remains of the old village stocks and the whipping post can still be found in this village and they were last used in 1860. On nearby Tarberry Hill there is said to be treasure left behind by Royalists on the run during the Civil War. While living here, novelist Anthony Trollope wrote four novels.

SHIP INN

The Ship Inn is a fine, four centuries old hostelry and was partly built from ships' timbers. Lord Nelson stayed here on occasion. There used to be a smugglers' passageway leading to the local cottages. There are two bars, one with a large open

fireplace and decorated with hunting scenes and horse brasses. It is a long, white building situated on a village corner.

WHITE HART INN

Opened 400 years ago, this is another of the haunted inns of Sussex. It is a two storey, white-painted, brick inn with three bars. There are stone steps leading up to the bars, which have beamed ceilings and inglenook fireplaces. It was once the home of the Old Club, the oldest known men's club in England, and every Whit Monday it is decorated with beech branches in memory of this. Looking east, there is a fine, spired church. Over the years there have been stories told of a strange man flitting between the bars.

Staplefield

(Map 3 page 8)

A staple or 'stapol' preceded the cross or 'crouche' as a marker for the Staple Hundred, a district division.

JOLLY TANNERS

In 1600, when Charles I was born, this inn opened opposite the present cricket green. It has been a coaching inn and there is a vast amount of brassware in the main bar and one smaller bar. There are a number of old photographs of the area on display. It was named after men in the leather tanning trade.

Steyning

(Map 4 page 8)

Steyning was recorded in AD 880 as 'aet Staeningum' and in 1086 as 'Staninges'. Born in AD 681, St Cuthman lived here with his paralysed mother. He pulled her about on a withy sledge. Some haymakers laughed at this, then a great flood came and ruined their hay, and, ever since then, it has always rained at haymaking in this field.

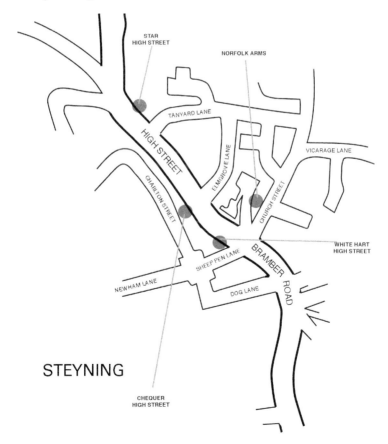

CHEQUER

Parts of the Chequer are over 500 years old. It is a large, white-painted, old coaching inn in the middle of the village, and it once held the town light. Throughout, there are several small, oak-beamed bars and at the side is the old coach entrance to the stables. Chequer is an ancient inn name that may have come from the Romans as there is evidence to suggest that it was used at Pompeii as a game similar to

draughts. Many pub games are still played here. The 18th-century inn sign is made from wrought iron and depicts a chequerboard. The sign was later used as a money table, which gave rise to the exchequer, a type of chessboard. It also indicated that the inn could be used for changing money or banking.

NORFOLK ARMS

There is a fine Jacobean staircase at this 17th-century inn and several nail studded doors. It is set in an area of 17th and 18th-century houses and is in the same street as the old grammar school. On the south side of the church are the original sanctuary rings. In mediaeval times a felon could hang on to such a ring and claim church protection, except if they had committed treason. There is also a portion of a Saxon grave said to have been that of King Ethelwulf.

STAR INN

The Star is a three centuries old hostelry once known as the Star of Bethlehem. Part of it was a Quaker-run home for waifs and strays. Features include farm implements and a collection of walking sticks. There is a series of small bars and cubbyholes named the Workshop, the Parlour and the Farmers' Bar.

WHITE HORSE INN

This name has been in constant use since the 15th century because of its heraldic connections and is in the top 10 of popular pub names. When a galloping white horse is used on the inn board it refers to the House of Hanover from the accession of George I in 1714. This is a town centre hotel covered in ivy and an old posting and coaching inn dating back to the 15th century. Oliver Cromwell stayed here.

St Leonards

(Map 7 page 10)

St Leonards is named after the patron saint of prisoners and was described in 1279 as 'Ecclesia Leonardi de Hastynges'.

BO-PEEP

This large corner pub near the sea front was first licensed in 1810 when it was called the New England Bank. The inn sign shows Little Bo-Peep on one side and smugglers on the other. The smuggling activities here led to a pitched battle, in 1828, with the revenue men. Once there was small window, high up on the pub, used as the lookout to watch for the revenue men, known as the 'bo-peep'. Builder James Burton started the building of the nearby St Leonard's garden city in 1828 and it was completed by his son, Decimus. James Burton's memorial is a pyramid to avoid the eastern curse, 'May jackasses sit on your father's grave'. The poet John Keats stayed here.

WISHING TREE

Wishing trees are not as well known as wishing wells. Anyone dropping a coin into such a well is carrying on the same belief that Celts had when they dropped human heads down wells to bring good luck and fortune. A two-year-old girl reported an apparition that was laughing but all she could say about it was, 'funny face'. Over the years there have been stories of curious bumping sounds and footsteps in an empty room. A middle-aged woman wearing early Victorian clothing has been spotted pushing a pram outside the pub.

Stopham Bridge

(Map 2 page 7)

Once occupied by Romans, in Saxon it was known as 'Stoppa ham', the home of Stoppa.

WHITE HART

Here there is a 14th-century bridge over the River Arun, and there has been a building on this site since before 1066. The inn is over 400 years old and is panelled and has low beams. As an inn sign, the white hart first became popular during the reign of Richard II, from 1377, as it was his heraldic symbol. All of his court and household wore it and tavern keepers used the sign to show their allegiance to that throne. It was Richard II who decreed that all inns should have a sign and said, 'Whosoever shall brew ale in the town with the intention of selling it must hang out a sign otherwise he shall forfeit his ale'. In 1807 a band of militia arrived here, threw the landlord into the river and drank his pub dry.

Storrington

(Map 2 page 7)

This village name came from 'Storca tun' or stork farm and was recorded as 'Storgetune' in 1086.

WHITE HORSE

The White Horse is a large inn on the main street opened in 1535, when Miles Coverdale published the first complete English Bible. Inside there are oak beams and a resident indwell, known for pushing and pulling at people. This is accompanied by chills and some curious noises. On one occasion, a letter was sent from a firm of solicitors to a guest, Sir Arnold Bax, Master of the King's Musick, who had died at the inn. It was, for some reason, put into his old room. Later it was recovered but with smudges all over it as though it had been read, although the room had been locked up all the time.

Thakeham

(Map 2 page 7)

The name comes from the Saxon 'Taec ham', meaning thatched roof, and was recorded as 'Tacaham' by 1073.

WHITE LION

The White Lion is a haunted pub that was once a smuggling centre. It opened in 1640 and was named after the heraldic insignia of Edward IV. The ghost here has been seen wearing an old-fashioned green cloak but there is no known story behind it. There were several miles of underground tunnels in this area, used to bring in smuggled booty. The smugglers terrorised the area from Goudhurst, Kent, through to Dorset. Villagers had to pay dues to them and were savagely beaten if they stepped out of line. The villagers of Goudhurst formed the Band of Militia to protect themselves and the local inns in Sussex and Kent. During a battle several smugglers were killed or injured. Later, local people gave evidence against the gang at Chichester Assizes and all were hanged. The pub was used by William Penn, a Quaker, as a meeting place as his family lived at Warminghurst.

Ticehurst

(Map 5 page 9)

This Saxon village was known as 'ticcenes hyrst', where young goats were grazed, and it translates as 'the kid's wood'.

BELL HOTEL

Part of the hotel dates back to 1296 and it became a coaching inn in the 14th century.

There is an inglenook fireplace with logs here. In 1292 the de Passele family built a moated manor near here, Pashley Manor. Later, it was bought by the Bulen family

from Norfolk, whose name became Boleyn, and Anne Boleyn stayed here in her childhood. In the church there is a collection of hand-embroidered kneeling stools showing life in the village.

BULL

The Bull is an old coaching inn with parts dating back over 600 years and a collection of 400 bells. The same family has been there for over half a century. About the time that Chaucer started his *Canterbury Tales*, a Wealden house was built on this site, made of timber with wattle and daub walls. This became the Bull and it now has flagged floors, long wooden tables and settles.

Tillington

(Map 2 page 7)

Tillington was recorded in a charter of AD 960 as 'Tullingtun'. It was the farm of a Saxon, 'Tulla'.

HORSE GUARDS INN

The Horse Guards is a delightful three centuries old inn on a hill with exposed beams, open fires, antique furniture, country-style prints and polo mallets on display. It was earlier named the Royal Horse Guards after a regiment stationed at Petworth Park during the Napoleonic wars. Once three cottages, it has been built into one bar and the front is accessed by a flight of stone steps.

Trotton

(Map 1 page 6)

From the 14th century, Trotton Bridge has spanned the Rother and was originally stepping stones set into the river bed. It was rebuilt by Thomas, Lord Camoys, who fought with Henry V at the Battle of Agincourt, and his wife, Elisabeth, who was Shakespeare's Gentle Kate in *Henry IV*.

KEEPERS ARMS

The pub is named after the gamekeepers on the local estate and is situated in a small village off the main road. It is near an ancient church with the oldest brass rubbings in the country. The inn has oak beams, oak panelling, a log fire and an eclectic collection of ornaments. On oak floors there are Turkish carpets with leather armchairs and a Moroccan lamp. There are ancient burial mounds nearby.

Uckfield

(Map 5 page 9)

From 'Ucca's feld', meaning Ucca's field, Uckfield was known as 'Ukkefeld' by 1220.

COCK AND BULL

This most unusually named pub is a large Victorian edifice opposite Uckfield railway station and is the only one in the country. The expression 'cock and bull' comes from two inns at Stony Stratford named the Cock and the Bull. Both rented out horses and each maintained that their horses were the best, hence cock and bull story. There is a local Cock and Bull Society that, some time ago, voted to break away from the main authority in Milton Keynes.

Udimore

(Map 7 page 10)

Udimore was named thus because of the intervention by the angels when the church was being built. As it was on marshy grounds, the angels kept moving the foundations and as they flew through the air carrying the stones they cried, as one, 'Over the mere-over the mere', which later became Udimore. However, it is also thought to come from the Saxon 'Udan mere' or Uda's Mere. The font in the local church was made of wood that is completely infra dig. The good (and parsimonious) parishioners painted an old pudding bowl to look like stone, using lead paint on the inside.

KINGS HEAD

Built in 1535 and extended in the 17th century, this pub is a bucolic imbiber's dream. It is beamed, has wooden floors and two open fires. The long, oak bar was installed in the 1930s. The inn is haunted by a curious ghost that moves furniture around late at night. In the 18th century, the parish council meetings were held at the Kings Head and the beer was paid for on the rates.

Upper Beeding

(Map 4 page 8)

KING'S ARMS

The pub was built in 1504 near St Mary's House, which was erected earlier, in about 1470, on the site of an old inn. This ancient inn had been used by pilgrims on their way to Canterbury. The King's Arms is on two storeys and has low-beamed bars and an incredible rear door.

Upper Dicker

(Map 6 page 9)

The name comes from the Latin 'dicora', meaning ten or a tenth, eventually becoming, in Old English, 'dyker' then 'dicker', meaning half a score especially when counting leather hides.

PLOUGH

The Plough was a farmhouse in 1641, just before the English Civil War. There are two main bars with oak beams, large inglenook fireplaces, log fires and deep sofas and armchairs. In the huge garden eating area there is a fish pond and an old-fashioned village pump built in over a well.

Vines Cross

This name was given to the village by an Elizabethan landowner, John Vyne, in 1596.

BREWER'S ARMS

The Brewer's Arms was built in 1753, the same year that the British Museum opened. There is a large collection of antiques in the bars including large, old bicycles, a

wheelbarrow and a piano suspended from the ceiling. There is also a large library of books for the delectation of the solitary drinker. The bucolic extravaganza continues into the lavatories, which are named Foxes and Vixens. Once the pub was called Clappers, but now only one bar is called that, after a wooden bridge with loose boards that went clap-clap as anyone crossed it. On the Clappers bar ceiling is a collection of large cups and saucers. At the local church there is a memorial to Richard Woodman, a local ironmaster, who was one of the ten Protestant Martyrs burned at Lewes in 1557. The Brewers started as a taproom and has been run by the same family for over 40 years.

Wadhurst

(Map 5 page 9)

From 'Wadas hyrst', meaning a wood hill, Wadhurst was recorded as 'Wadehurt' in 1253. On 8 December 1863 the last great bare-knuckle fight took place here between Tom King, an Englishman, and an American called Heenan. Heenan weighed 15 stones and King, 14 stones. It went for 36 rounds and King eventually won. At the time, the public were dismayed by the fight and demands rose for such fighting to be banned.

GREYHOUND

The Greyhound is a five centuries old former coaching inn and was once the haunt of the Hawkhurst Gang. Some pubs called the Greyhound are named after a famous mail coach or the heraldic device of the Dukes of Newcastle. In the middle ages a greyhound was known as a gazehound because it relied on sight rather than hearing when used in hunting. It is part-panelled and has a fine collection of artifacts, a

rocking chair and a padded settle near the inglenook fireplace. Pub entertainment consists of ring-the-bull, shove ha'penny and bar billiards.

BEST BEECH INN
The oldest part of this pub was built in 1640, when Star Chamber was phased out. An elderly male ghost is seen near here carrying a large sack. He wears a long brown coat and walks along the road before disappearing into an old gateway. Legend has it that it is the ghost of a poacher or apple thief, shot by a gamekeeper in the early 1800s.

Walderton

(Map 1 page 6)

It has been called this since 1167 and in Saxon was named 'Wealdere tun', meaning the farm of a forest warrior.

BARLEYMOW
A mow was the rural word for a stack and barley is the main ingredient of beer so the combined name indicated that this was a pub. Originally this pub was a pair of cottages dating from about 1740. There are several bars with original stone-flag floors and a wood-burning stove and many old photographs and documents are on display.

Waldron

(Map 6 page 9)

In Saxon days this was a heavily wooded area and the village was named 'Weald earn', the forest house.

STAR INN
As the Pilgrim Fathers set sail for the Americas in 1620 the Star opened its doors as an inn. The large open bar has old oak beams and a large fireplace

and fireback dated 1694. The Star is hidden away down quiet country lanes, on a village square with a war memorial and the open bar has solid oak beams.

Warbleton

(Map 6 page 9)

The name comes from the Saxon, 'Waerburh tun', meaning a woman's farm.

WAR-BILL-IN-TUN
A bill was the word for several different kinds of sword-like weapons so this pub name is a play on this and the village name. The original inn was 13th-century and

it is first recorded as having an innkeeper in 1642, at the outbreak of the English Civil War. Then it was described as the Two Tuns. Once a two-storey, brick and tile building, it was rebuilt in 1969. It is haunted by Richard Woodman, a Sussex iron-founder, who was burned at the stake in Lewes as a heretic. Woodman had called his Rector 'Mr Facing-both-ways' for being a Protestant under Henry VIII and a Catholic under Queen Mary. He took refuge here before he was captured.

157

Warnham

(Map 3 page 8)

In Saxon times this was a heavily wooded area known as 'Weald aern', meaning forest house.

GREETS INN

The Greets is a roadside inn that was once a farmhouse and is over 500 years old. It is tiled and timbered and has an inglenook fireplace. The inn sign shows two old friends greeting each other. It is near Warnham War Museum, which houses a display of memorabilia of the two wars including a NAFFI tea wagon.

Wartling

(Map 6 page 9)

The name is of Saxon origin from the settlement of 'Wyrtel's' people. An early radar station was built nearby.

LAMB INN

First recorded in 1534, when Peter's Pence, the annual offering to the Pope, was abolished, the Lamb was not recorded as an inn until 1771. It is a white-painted, two-storey building, surrounded by trees, with tiled floors, nooks and crannies and three open fires. It is rumoured that there were tunnels between the inn and nearby church, used for smuggling. In the 1900s Rudyard Kipling travelled to Wartling to have a meal here.

Washington

(Map 4 page 8)

The village was named 'Wasa-ing-tun', meaning the settlement of the sons of Wasa. A legend says that treasure is buried near the village but it is guarded by the ghost of an old, white-bearded man seen wandering in the fields. At Chancton Farm, nearby, a pot of Saxon coins was unearthed by a plough in 1866. In an early guide to the village, Revd John Evans said: 'Here is nothing attractive excepting its rural position'.

FRANKLAND ARMS

It is a large roadside village inn, situated next door to a tiny post office. Behind one of the inglenook fireplaces here there is a light lit by natural gas. Since 1795, this pub was known as the Washington Inn. Recently, it was renamed after William Frankland of Muntham Court, Findon. He was the son of a Governor of Bengal and made a three-year journey back to England through Constantinople, over 200 years ago. Frankland became well known for designing appliances to be used for scientific purposes.

West Ashling

(Map 1 page 6)

RICHMOND ARMS

This name refers to the Dukes of Richmond, and earliest records of this building date back to 1780 when it was called Waterbeach House. Across the road is the site of the old village cockpit. This was also the site of the last bare-knuckle fight in this country (although this is claimed by a pub in Yorkshire called the Bareknuckle Boys where such fights were still taking place in the 1930s). In the village there are old cottages and a millpond. There are two rare black swans here. The Roman satirist Juvenal referred to the black swan as a 'rara avis', meaning a rare bird. The black swan became a popular name for pubs in the 16th century to indicate that the landlord himself was a rare bird. On the walls of this pub there are numbered wooden ducks used for duck racing.

West Chitlington

(Map 2 page 7)

West Chitlington was known as 'Cillingtun' in AD 969, meaning a high place. Old Dame Jackson was the witch of the village and cured earache, toothache, stomach ache and rheumatism, using oil extracted from adders that cost her one penny each. The pillory and stocks from 1650 have been rebuilt outside the parish church.

ELEPHANT AND CASTLE

Forget 'Infanta de Castile' as the legend behind this pub's name; it was named after the Cutler's Company of 1623 whose crest was an elephant with a howdah on its back that looked like a small castle. In Victorian times, cockney rhyming slang used 'elephants' to mean drunk, from elephant's trunk. This is another delightful, old-fashioned country pub with low and exposed beams. It even has its own golfing society. This pub was well connected with the smuggling gangs and contraband was hidden in the false window sills here. Surrounded by pine trees, this stone-built pub dates back over three centuries and outside it has waterfowl ponds and an aviary.

FIVE BELLS

The Five Bells is a treasure that can be found in Smock Alley down Haglands or Roundabout Lane, outside the village. Five bells used to mean, in Royal Navy terms,

2.30pm or closing time for pubs until a few years ago. This is a fine roadside inn with a racy clientele.

West Dean

(Map 1 page 6)

HURDLEMAKERS

Named after local hurdle makers, this pub opened in 1755 for those who made the mobile wicker fencing for farmers. It was once called the Star and Garter after the most noble Order of the Garter, instituted by Edward III in 1348. There are Celtic fields above the village and round barrows from the Bronze Age.

West Firle

(Map 6 page 9)

The name is from the Saxon 'fierol', meaning oak covered land. Firle Beacon was a site used to raise the alarm for the Spanish Armada and an armed horseman guarded the brushwood here against vandals setting fire to it. There is still a working forge in the village.

RAM INN

This pub name is often found where there is a local wool business. A ram has appeared on the sign of the Worshipful Company of Clothworkers since the 14th century. This Ram is a five centuries old, former coaching inn once used as a courthouse for local criminals. Many ancient features are still on display at the inn. One couple, George and Mary Hafflett, ran this pub for 77 years, but when they left in 1985 they took away the original brass till, which was still able to give change for a sovereign. It is haunted by a young girl who was found dead in the attic. She had been living rough and had a deformed leg so the landlord took her in. Sounds of her limping up a narrow stairway to the room where she died have been heard in the pub. The pub name is also part of the heraldry of Sir John Gage, vice-chancellor to Henry VIII, whose family introduced the greengage to England. Another famous Gage was Thomas who was Commander-in-Chief of the British forces in America during the War of Independence in 1775. Local societies perform traditional Sussex music here.

Westham

(Map 6 page 9)

The name originated from west enclosure in Saxon and it was known as 'Westhamme' by 1252.

PEVENSEY CASTLE

The Pevensey Castle is a village centre pub named after the local castle. The ruins of Pevensey Castle are haunted by Roman soldiers who are heard fighting and crashing about and also by Lady Jane Pelham, who defended the castle against an army while her husband was away fighting in the 14th century. The same Pelham captured the French king by taking a grip on his belt buckle at Poitiers in 1356 and was allowed to incorporate a buckle into his family coat of arms by Edward III. The nearby church of St Mary the Virgin was the first church built by the Normans in this country in 1080 and it contains a fragment of King Solomon's Temple, brought back by the Revd Howard Hopley in 1860. William Leeke, a former curate at the church, was a Standard Bearer at the Battle of Waterloo. In the church graveyard is a plague stone for the victims of the Black Death. The 14th-century Old Mint House in the town is haunted by a young girl, murdered 400 years ago.

West Hoathly

(Map 3 page 8)

Sometimes pronounced West 'Holy' by older residents, the name comes from the Saxon 'Haeo leah', meaning a clearing of the heathland, and it was first recorded in AD 765.

CAT INN

This is a large village pub opposite the church. It has a vast inglenook fireplace with a log-burning grate and a seat at each side. It is tile-hung and has white brickwork. Nearby there are some 17th-century cottages that are also tile-hung. On the run from the fencibles (a band of retired soldiers) following a vicious murder, a man, Jacob Hirsch, appeared here seeking refuge in 1734. It was a haunt of smugglers and he thought he would be safe here. He noticed the landlady, Mary Brooks, watching him and then realised he had blood coating his sleeve so he made off again. This time he hid up a chimney in a nearby manor house but the fencibles turned up and started a fire. Hirsch collapsed in the smoke, fell down on to the flames and was arrested. Later he was hanged and his body was cut up and taken to Wivelsfield where it was strung up on a gibbet. This became known as Jacob's Post, and people would travel miles to cut slivers of wood from it as they believed it to be curative. His ghost turns up at the Cat Inn occasionally, as a man with wide staring eyes, seen in the bar, with blood on his old-fashioned jacket.

WHITE HART

The White Hart is over 600 years old and was formerly a tythe barn. It was visited by Charles II on several hunting occasions. It has an inglenook fireplace for wintertime

fires. It is a half-timbered, wayside inn and has stood on the turnpike road since the 14th century. Part of it was once a mead-maker's cottage. Inside is a police poster offering a £250 reward for the capture of Dr Harvey Crippen and Ethel Neve, from 1910, wanted for murder and mutilation. Nearby is the Priests House, the local museum of village life and Wakehurst, a Royal botanic garden.

Whatlington

(Map 7 page 10)

Whatlington was a Saxon farmstead of the 'Hwaetelingas'.

ROYAL OAK

The Royal Oak is a four centuries old hostelry with a baronial hall and an 80ft deep well inside. A delightful old pub on the village green, it is a white-painted, weatherboarded building.

Wineham

(Map 3 page 8)

ROYAL OAK

The pub features a collection of pottery, old cork screws and beer drawn from a cask behind the bar. Originally a cottage dating back to the 14th century, it has black and white timbering and a half-stable door to get into the bars. It has been in the same family for over 50 years. There is an enormous, log burning, inglenook fireplace.

Willingdon

(Map 6 page 9)

Saxons called this 'Willa dun', meaning Willa's down, and became 'Willendone' by 1086, and this is still the local pronunciation.

RED LION

This Red Lion was used in George Orwell's *Animal Farm*, where the old farmer drank, and it is the third pub to have been on the site. The name is one of those generic ones for pubs that came from John of Gaunt in the 14th century. It once had a mangle room where local washerwomen would wring out clothes for a penny a bundle.

There is still an old village hand pump opposite the alms houses. There are two large bars with photographs of the old village on the walls.

WHEATSHEAF

This has been a popular pub name since the 17th century and appears on the coat of arms of the Worshipful Company of Bakers (from 1486) and on that of the Brewers' Company. Once two cottages, the pub was built in the 17th century and was part of the Willingdon Estate. There are two bars with extensive eating areas.

Wilmington

(Map 6 page 9)

The name originates from the Saxon 'Winel tone', meaning the homestead of Winel, becoming 'Wineltone' in the Domesday Book. Burial mounds have been found here, on the downs. It was owned by Earl Godwin, father of King Harold. The churchyard yew tree is said to be 2,000 years old and now needs wooden poles for support.

GIANT'S REST

The Giant's Rest is a village inn named after the Long Man of Wilmington, a nearby chalk figure that is 226ft high. This is cut into the chalk of Windover Hill. Very little is known of the history of the Long Man and several different dates for it have been given. However, in 1874 it was given its present shape because it had become overgrown. The Giant's Rest was formerly called the Black Horse. The pub has regular exhibitions by local artists.

Winchelsea

(Map 7 page 10)

One mile south of here is the Old Winchelsea that was destroyed by the sea in 1287. The present village is part-walled and one of the most attractive in Sussex.

BRIDGE INN

An attractive inn on the roadside below Winchelsea, this pub started life as an ale-house over 500 years ago. It has low beams and open fires. During battles between local smugglers and revenue men, one smuggler was carried into the yard here where he died. There have been tales over the years that he is still in residence and makes an appearance from time to time.

NEW INN

Here John Wesley gave his last open air sermon under a tree outside the pub, in 1790. The tree stood here until 1927, then a new one was planted from a cutting. During the 14th and 15th centuries, this area was pillaged by the French. In 1359 3,000 of them arrived and burned down houses, farms and churches and murdered everyone they could find. Nearby is Deadman's Lane where no birds sing and local legend has

it that many souls from that dreadful day still dwell there. Centuries later, smugglers hid their booty under gravestones at the church. Two infamous highwaymen lived at an old Franciscan monastery in the town, George and Joseph Weston, who were caught robbing the Bristol Mail and were hanged at Tyburn in 1782. They are still believed to be in Winchelsea and have been seen hiding under trees as if waiting to pillage and steal. Galloping hooves have been heard on local roads.

Wisborough Green

(Map 2 page 7)

In the Middle Ages, the Huguenots came to Wisborough Green and set up glass-making factories. The church was a place of pilgrimage because of the holy relics inside including St Thomas Becket's cloak.

BAT AND BALL

Originally a 16th-century farmhouse, it is now an elegant 18th-century building with a Victorian drapery shop built within the bars. The name does not always refer to cricket but sometimes to Hellfire Clubs from the early 18th century. Their members met in a circular building and their emblem was a bat flying around a sphere to show their nocturnal and very racy activities. There is a huge garden here and camping facilities. There are records of cricket being played with a curved bat and a single stump on the large green before the pub. Once 1,000 fish were stocked in the local pond and a wary eye kept watch for herons.

CRICKETERS ARMS

Overlooking the village green that is home to local cricketers, it is a fine looking inn with wood block floors and a wood burning stove. The green is also home to English motor mower racing and hot air ballooning, especially in August. On the east side of the huge green is the Zoar, a chapel dating from 1753.

THREE CROWNS

The Three Crowns is a five centuries old roadside pub just off the village green and next to the village pond. There are several small bars with wood panels and exposed beams. Today Three Crowns is an unusual name, referring to the three wise men who visited Jesus in the stable or to James I when he became the first king of England, Scotland and Wales. It was the heraldic sign of the Worshipful Company of Drapers in 1364.

Withyham

(Map 5 page 9)

Withyham is a village between two willow-shaded streams, originally called 'wiogig hamm'.

DORSET ARMS

In 1556, when Thomas Cranmer, Archbishop of Canterbury, was burned at the stake for heresy and Anne of Cleves died, this pub opened. A completely unspoiled pub, it has low ceilings and a floor of unvarnished local oak. It was originally called Somers Farm and the first tenant was Edward Burrist. In 1677 one landlord was fined for running an illegal alehouse.

Wivelsfield

(Map 3 page 8)

Recorded in AD 765 as 'Wifelsfeld', Wivelsfield had become known as 'Wyvelsfield' by the early 1400s.

FOX AND HOUNDS

A large roadside inn, once called the Anchor, near the old turnpike road, the Fox and Hounds is over 300 years old. It was an alehouse and is haunted by two ghosts. One, 'Fred', a rather battered looking old gentleman, has been seen sitting in an armchair in the bar and throws bottles about occasionally. The female ghost has been seen wearing a grey dress in the ladies' lavatory.

ROYAL OAK

The Royal Oak is a tile-hung and brick roadside inn, and it was once called Jacob's Cross after a felon executed here for murder. Jacob Hirsh, a travelling pedlar, murdered two people and tried to kill the landlord, Richard Miles, then escaped to East Hoathly. Many years ago a woman and her daughter heard excited sounds

coming from one part of a room here. When looking at a wall mirror they saw a large religious-style cross appear on it, describing it as dark grey and slightly misty, and it remained there for some time before disappearing. A manager awoke at four in the morning and saw a woman in a long white dress, grey shawl and old-fashioned hair net. She was pushing at what had been a door many years ago, and since bricked up, and then disappeared through it.

Wivelsfield Green

(Map 3 page 8)

COCK INN

Once known as the Fighting Cock when there was a cockpit nearby, this pub was used by smugglers as a halfway house between London and Brighton. Since the

1940s, there have been stories of objects being thrown around rooms with tremendous force and cold areas within the pub. Curtains have come away from their rings and been left on the floor in crumpled heaps. One landlord woke up when he heard a window screech as it opened during the night. Upon investigation, he found the window had locks on it but it was wide open. When trying to close it, he found it had been forced open so violently he could not do so. Another manager awoke to see the apparition of a woman dressed in white cross his room and disappear through a wall. She has also been spotted in the bar as she walks across and again disappears through a solid wall.

Yapton

(Map 2 page 7)

Originally Yapton was known as 'Eabba tun' or 'Eappa' after one of the four disciples of St Wilfrid who brought Christianity to Sussex in the seventh century. The phrase 'Do you come from Yapton?', meaning that someone has left the door open, comes from here as smugglers going through the village might have needed to hide from the revenue men so the doors were left open. However, another story of its origins says that a rich man blocked up his windows here to avoid paying window tax, but it was so dark that servants had to leave the doors open to see. Occasionally there have been ghostly sounds of a polka being played in lanes leading to the village.

MAYPOLE INN

Down a narrow lane from the village, this small flint-built pub, first licensed in 1783, was built from two cottages beside a main road. The road was cut off when the railways came in 1846 and it has remained isolated ever since. There are many country pubs named the Maypole after the sites of ancient maypoles that date back to pagan times. Decorated with banners and streamers, people danced around it on May Day and elected a May Queen. This was, at one time, banned by the Puritans.

SHOULDER OF MUTTON AND CUCUMBER

This is a fine, large roadside village inn and it is located opposite a fascinating country antiques shop. A shoulder of mutton was a popular dish at inns in coaching days. At this pub they served it with a cucumber sauce giving it its unique name. In 1759 landlord William Verrell gave his recipe for the sauce: 'Cut into quarters, fry with butter and add stock, chopped parsley and lemon juice.' In 1898 a Yapton thatcher called Marley sold his wife to the local ratcatcher for 7s 6d and a quart of beer.

ND - #0312 - 270225 - C0 - 210/148/11 - PB - 9781780911892 - Gloss Lamination